"A thoughtful documentation of one woman's struggle to maintain her ancestral homeland."
—*Booklist*

"Marsh makes commendable use of the scant documentary evidence to piece together Hannah Freeman's life. Her painstaking efforts to give Hannah a voice are impressive."
—Thomas Britten, *The Historian*

"The book is engagingly written—and impassioned as Marsh clearly chastises Hannah Freeman's Quaker neighbors for their hypocrisy in promoting friendly relations with indigenous neighbors and landowners, while facilitating their dispossession."
—Gunlog Fur, *Journal of the Early Republic*

"In a genre that so often focuses on the lives of politically significant 'great men' (and occasionally women), we rarely learn of the lives of the marginalized, but this is exactly what historian Dawn G. Marsh has attempted—*A Lenape among the Quakers* is a scathing indictment of the hypocrisy of Quakers' professions of peace while engaged in a land grab. . . . This book will prove useful for those interested in the history of colonial British America, women's history, ethnohistory, and the history of memory."
—Michelle LeMaster, *Ethnohistory*

"With great insight and sensitivity, Dawn Marsh has pieced together Hannah Freeman's story. All who have ever wondered what happened to Pennsylvania's Native people should read this book."
—Nancy Shoemaker, author of *A Strange Likeness: Becoming Red and White in Eighteenth-Century North America*

"Using the closely examined life of a single eighteenth-century Native American woman, Dawn Marsh convincingly challenges Pennsylvania's claim to a more just and humane treatment of its indigenous peoples, persuasively contending that Native Americans adopted complex strategies to preserve their cultural heritage, and explores the significance of the continuing mythology of 'Indian Hannah' Freeman—all in a good read."
—Melton McLaurin, author of *Celia, a Slave*

A Lenape among the Quakers

A Lenape among the Quakers

The Life of Hannah Freeman

DAWN G. MARSH

University of Nebraska Press
Lincoln & London

Parts of this book have previously appeared in different
form in "Hannah Freeman: Gendered Sovereignty in Penn's
Peaceable Kingdom," in *Gender and Sovereignty in Indigenous
North America, 1400–1850*, ed. Sandra Slater and Fay A.
Yarborough (Columbia: University of South Carolina Press,
2011), 102–22.

Library of Congress Cataloging-in-Publication Data
Marsh, Dawn G.
A Lenape among the Quakers: the life of Hannah Freeman /
Dawn G. Marsh.
pages cm.
Includes bibliographical references.
ISBN 978-0-8032-4840-3 (cloth: alk. paper)—
ISBN 978-0-8032-7520-1 (paper: alk. paper)—
ISBN 978-0-8032-5419-0 (epub)—
ISBN 978-0-8032-5420-6 (mobi)—
ISBN 978-0-8032-5418-3 (pdf)
1. Freeman, Hannah, 1730–1802. 2. Delaware women—
Pennsylvania—Chester County—Biography. 3. Delaware
Indians—Missions—Pennsylvania—Chester County. 4.
Quakers—Missions—Pennsylvania—Chester County. I. Title.
E99.D2F746 2014
974.8'00497345092—dc23
[B]
2013031268

Set in ITC New Baskerville by Hannah Gokie.

For
the Lenape people
and
Jesse, Whitney, and Harper

PUBLICATION OF THIS BOOK
IS SUPPORTED BY A GRANT FROM
Jewish Federation of Greater Hartford

Contents

Illustrations

Acknowledgments

This book began over a decade ago with my discovery of two eighteenth-century documents that inspired me with an inexplicable obsession to "unsilence" Hannah Freeman's story. I did not understand how far or how long that journey would take, but I have no regrets about my choice. I am wiser for the journey, but not weary, and my obsession is now a passion. Hannah Freeman taught me quite a few lessons along the way, and there is much work yet to do.

There are far too many friends and colleagues who offered support and enthusiasm along the way to name individually. Please know that you are deeply appreciated and forever have a seat at my table. However, there are a few who must be named. The first are my children: Jesse Preston Otawka, Whitney Morgan Otawka, and Harper Mackenzie Valentine Otawka. They were the first reasons I embarked on the more difficult of the paths available. They continue to inspire me to be a better human being. Jesse gave me his steadfast loyalty and strength throughout the most difficult times. His sense of humor, kind heart, and compassion kept us together. He is *my* superhero. My oldest daughter, Whitney, inspired me to never let go. Her tenacity and her passion for her own career remind me how lucky we are to be doing work that we love, and her exuberance and joy teach me to enjoy the ride. Finally, Harper, a gifted writer and poet, reinvigorated my own aspirations as a writer. Her love of language and words are always with me. Her empathy for those suffering injustice reminds me that words are powerful weapons we must use wisely.

Professional support came from many sources. Sharon Salinger and Rebecca "Monte" Kugel recognized capabilities I had not yet discovered in myself and provided intellectual space and support during my graduate program at the University of California, Riverside. Laurie and Diane Rofini and the staff at the Chester County Historical Society and Chester County Archives introduced me to the Albert Cook Meyers Collection and more. Their expert insights were invaluable. There are many colleagues past and present who listened and advised along the way, but several stand out and must be noted: Helen Hornbeck Tanner, Susan Sleeper Smith, Theda Perdue, and Nancy Shoemaker—trailblazers all. My thanks go also to Matt Bokovoy, who recognized the importance of Hannah's story. His mentoring made me a far better storyteller. I must also thank the Philips Fund for Native American Research administered through the American Philosophical Society, which provided the seed money for the project, and acknowledge the generous support of the Library Scholars Grants at Purdue University and the Purdue Research Foundation Grant, which provided crucial funds during revisions of the manuscript.

A few final acknowledgments go to my new extended family in Lafayette, Indiana. I accepted an appointment at Purdue University in 2007 under the most trying and difficult of personal circumstances. In a very short time and with very little effort I found myself surrounded with good friends, both on campus and off. I cooked, you ate—you shared your families, and I shared mine. We laughed, argued, teased, and hugged. Some moved on and are missed dearly, but new friends continue to enter my life. All of you eased my transition from Californian to midwesterner and continue to help me call this strange and marvelous place home. You know who you are. A finer group of miscreants and charlatans cannot be found.

A Lenape among the Quakers

Introduction

On July 28, 1797, Hannah Freeman, an elderly indigent Lenape woman, stood before Moses Marshall, Chester County's newly appointed almsman, and delivered a brief account of her life; two hundred years later one anthropologist credited it as a Native American biography "that predates by nearly one hundred years the earliest Native American story now known."[1] But few historians note her existence as anything more than incidental to the larger narrative of Pennsylvania history and eighteenth-century indigenous-white relations. However, Hannah Freeman's story plays a critical role in the popular construction of Pennsylvania's past on a regional level and provides a portal to examination of the complex dynamics of indigenous-white relations in eighteenth-century North America more generally. A careful study of Hannah Freeman gives us an opportunity to critique the colonialist memorials to her life spent among the Quakers but, more important, her life merits attention because it is a story of Lenape survivance that demonstrates the means by which she and other indigenous peoples found new ways to live in their historic homelands despite the enormous pressures of colonization.[2]

The story of Hannah Freeman is an imperfect history. The paucity of primary documentary evidence and the generational layers of oral accounts, family histories, and intentional silences make the endeavor of unearthing her story all the more daunting. The effort is worth it because Hannah Freeman's experiences as a Native American woman living deeply entrenched in a colonial settler community challenge our understanding of Indian-white interactions beyond the borderlands, frontiers, and middle grounds that are usually addressed in scholarship. Her experiences and the accounts by those who knew her offer an alternate history of a colonial community during a century of upheaval and transformation that enveloped all who lived through it.

Hannah Freeman's life story provides a valuable perspective on several levels of Pennsylvania, colonial, and women's history. Her role as the "last of her kind" in southeastern Pennsylvania gave regional historians critical proof that indigenous peoples in Pennsylvania vanished with her death.[3] This belief held sway in the region from a generation after her death to the present. The power of this communal memory, the extent to which the region's residents continue to protect, commemorate, and preserve that story, begs to be reevaluated since it conceals day-to-day realities of others like Hannah who refused to abandon their homelands and their indigenous identities. The complexities of interdependencies, obligations, and kinshiplike adaptations are made visible in a close study of the intimate exchanges between Hannah Freeman and her neighboring Quakers. Further, analysis brings to light the ways in which her Quaker neighbors, despite their most benevolent and pacifist intentions, dispossessed Native peoples of their lands. Subsequently, construction of this founding myth, which lauded William Penn's "peaceable kingdom," erased Hannah Freeman and the histories of other Native peoples, who were hiding in plain sight. The peaceable kingdom was, after all, a violent place. Today Pennsylvania remains one of the few states in the nation lacking a federally recognized tribe.

On a broader national scale, a reexamination of Lenape diplomatic strategies from the period that predates William Penn's arrival until Hannah's lifetime reveals a history of complex and initially successful tactics that ultimately failed the larger Lenape community in the face of the Quaker colonial regime and the demographics of European colonization. Both the Walking Purchase Treaty (1737) and the Paxton Massacre (1763) stand out as violent and coercive exceptions to the mythologized "peaceable kingdom," often making their way into historical narratives as tragic anomalies in the colony's history.[1] At first glance these violent episodes suggest a less than peaceful indigenous-white experience in colonial Pennsylvania, but most often they are explained away as dark stains on an otherwise pacific past of Native-white relations. Both occurred in Hannah's lifetime and played some part in her personal life as well as in the destiny of her people. The experiences of Hannah and her family in the largely Quaker community in which they resided shed new light on the problematic nature of even the most benevolently intentioned colonial systems.

Hannah's story ultimately broadens our understanding of the gendered experience of Native Americans in colonial Pennsylvania and offers testimony of the economic transformation of women's labor in southeastern Pennsylvania that initiated the exclusion of marginalized female populations (single women, Native women, and free black women). Colonial institutions and ideologies eroded traditional indigenous economic and social assets, even though this was not expressly a goal of the colonial mercantilist system. When placed within the context of this larger economic landscape, Hannah's experience testifies to the persistence of traditional matrilineal networks that remained invisible to the dominant settler society.

Hannah Freeman's story is a history burdened with paradoxes. Peace reigned between Hannah Freeman and her Quaker neighbors as the violent events of the eighteenth century engulfed the region: the French and Indian War, the Paxton Massacre, and American Revolution. Hannah and her neighbors remained uniquely separate in their cultural histories, traditions, and practices but at the same time had much in common. They farmed, worked, and had families side by side. They healed sickness, shared loss, and buried their dead in ways that created mutual empathy, facilitating Hannah Freeman's lifetime residence in the Brandywine River valley. Quakers frequently opened their fields and farmlands to seasonal Lenape occupation and allowed loose access to resources traditionally fenced and defined by fee simple deeds. Yet Hannah and the Lenapes understood their community and land as more malleable and timeless than the Quaker settlers, who maintained a more fixed and temporal understanding of property and society. Although these conflicting perceptions eventually led to the Lenapes' permanent dispossession, they also inspired Hannah Freeman's tenacious claims to her homeland. Perhaps the most difficult paradox this research considers is the concurrent story of disappearance and survival, a paradox that is not unique to Hannah Freeman's experience in eighteenth-century Pennsylvania but can be found in the histories of small towns and agricultural counties throughout the United States.[5]

The greatest challenge to illuminating Hannah Freeman's story is the silence of the historical record. Regional scholars dismiss Hannah Freeman's story as more myth than history, hardly deserving of their attention. Hannah is regarded as a colorful character to be pitied rather than a unique and complicated "voice" in the historical narrative. This book challenges such assumptions about Hannah Freeman's story not only by paying closer attention to the details of her day-to-day existence but by examining how her Quaker neighbors and the colonial government responded to her persistent presence on a landscape they increasingly claimed as their own. Further, this story moves Native American women's history away from a narrative of loss and victimization toward a framework of resistance and adaptation. What was the impact of western European economic systems on women's roles in Native societies, particularly in Hannah Freeman's case? Many authors argue that the introduction of market capitalism into Native North America altered economic roles through a loss of power. It is an assimilationist argument that subtly suggests inevitability. In this perspective,

Hannah Freeman emerges as a tragic figure, overwhelmed by the mercantilist system introduced by European colonists. Recent studies of indigenous women in North America suggest they adapted gender-defined economic activities and subsistence strategies in response to the changes ushered in by colonial systems not out of desperation but in order to take full advantage of the new market economy. This did not lead to a loss of power but instead cultivated the necessary support for a continued independent and productive place in these newly formed societies, sustained by traditional kinship structures and resources.[6] Considered within this framework, Hannah Freeman's story emerges as a story of resilience and continuity.

Three books deserve mention because they are instrumental in how I understand my work and professional obligations as a historian of Native American and indigenous history. The first, Laurel Thatcher Ulrich's *Midwife's Tale: The Life of Martha Ballard, Based on Her Diary, 1785–1812*, taught me the importance and meaning of the stories of ordinary women. What some see as the mundane and insignificant can be crucial, in the right hands, in understanding our history. The second, *Silencing the Past: The Power and Production of History* by Michel-Rolph Trouillot, galvanized my commitment to problematize Pennsylvania's "peaceable kingdom" and try to give Hannah Freeman and the Lenape people a more nuanced voice in that narrative. Finally, *Decolonizing Methodologies: Research and Indigenous Peoples* by Linda Tuhiwai Smith laid the foundation for my own professional research ethics and obligations in relation to my work with Native American and indigenous communities.

This story attempts to write the silences of Hannah Freeman's life and present an intimate portrait of an indigenous woman, the importance of the cultural legacy she inherited from her people, and the vital role that legacy played in the choices she made when faced by the changes introduced by one brand of English colonialism. Why did the Quakers allow Hannah Freeman and other Native Americans to stay on their lands when vigilante attacks and war made it difficult for them to do so? Hannah Freeman never converted to Quakerism, nor is there evidence that her neighbors tried to convert her. Why not? Quakers' missionary effort to "civilize" American Indians was a keystone of their institutional programs. And why, above all else, was it important for the residents of Chester County to claim that Hannah Freeman was the "last of her kind"? Perhaps a better question is: Why is this idea still important in the twenty-first century?

This is an easier story to ignore than it is to investigate and make sense of, but in the absence of direct evidence the historian is left with a choice. Too often the choice leaves the histories of women like Hannah Freeman untold and silenced. In the absence of sufficient documentary evidence, Hannah's story depends largely on the contextual events happening around her, the memories of those who knew her, and the "needles in a haystack" found in a broad array of colonial sources. If we are to understand anything about her life and the lives of Indian peoples living in Pennsylvania, particularly Indian women living in colonial Pennsylvania, then we must allow her story utterance and center it in the larger colonial and national narrative. No matter how distant or elevated in their political importance, these events pulled Hannah Freeman into a vortex of disruption and loss that touched her life on the most personal level. This study challenges the reader to consider a more holistic view of the indigenous experience and consider the Indian peoples who stopped fighting and stayed behind the highly contested lines and borders of "civilization." Their experiences are an understudied aspect of Native American history and deserve our fullest attention in order to lift them out of the shadows of myth and legend and into plain sight.

CHAPTER ONE

The Examination of Hannah Freeman

The appearance of Hannah Freeman, an elderly Lenape woman, standing on the West Chester courthouse steps on July 28, 1797, must have seemed a strange sight to those who took notice that day. At the end of the eighteenth century, eastern Pennsylvanians were far removed from the violent borders of Indian country in western Ohio. The great diaspora of Lenape communities who had called southeastern Pennsylvania home was not more than a half century in the past. Most residents believed that Pennsylvania's Indian population was long gone, and the sight of one old Lenape woman, if noticed at all, would provoke no more than a passing curiosity in those who saw her. But maybe some did take notice. Her dress was not unlike that of her neighbors, but there was no mistaking her indigenous identity. One neighbor described the elderly Hannah as a tall, lean woman with remarkable features that caused those who knew her to consider her a formidable personality.[1] Her copper-colored skin and white hair coupled with her stature and comportment may have caused a few heads to turn that hot summer day. Hannah was a Lenape woman and Pennsylvanians recalled her people as a remarkably graceful people of few words.

It is likely some townspeople recognized "Indian Hannah" and knew her as a neighbor and friend. She had spent her almost whole life in Chester County, and her life story wove through the memories and recollections of many of Chester County's most illustrious families, including the Marshalls, Barnards, Brintons, and Harlans. In recent decades Hannah had worked

1. Hannah Freeman memorial marker, 1909. (Author's collection)

for many of the local farm families, spinning flax and making baskets and brooms. When their children were sick local farmers sought Hannah's indigenous medical knowledge rather than consult the local physician. Her closest neighbors entrusted the care of their children to Hannah, and these same neighborhood children were probably frequent visitors to her cabin in the woods. Sometimes they came on errands for their parents, bringing supplies to Hannah in her later years. Hannah Baldwin fondly remembered the nickname the old Lenape woman had bestowed upon her, Betsy My-Eye, because the little girl had one blue eye and one brown one, just like Hannah. She also had a sense of humor, reportedly laughing when a friend showed her a machine-stitched broom, which she undoubtedly deemed inferior to her own handcrafted brooms. Many of Hannah's neighbors remembered the elderly woman as a welcome guest in their homes. She would spend days working beside with her Quaker sisters whom, like Hannah, farmers hired for seasonal work. But at the end of the day, unlike most other women, Hannah preferred to sit in the warmth of

The Examination of Hannah Freeman

the open stone hearth and smoke her pipe. It was a familiar and comforting memory cherished by the families who knew Hannah Freeman.[2]

Possibly Hannah Freeman reminded some townspeople of other, similarly named native residents who appear like shadows in local recollections: "Indian Betty," "Indian Pete," and "Indian Mary." Their irregular appearances at markets or along the country roads walking door-to-door peddling baskets and brooms grew less frequent as the century drew to an end. Hannah may have caused passersby to wonder where those few native neighbors were, what had become of them. They may have remembered the young Lenape boys who occasionally put on public displays of their hunting skills by accepting dares to shoot targets and who most often bested their colonial challengers. Perhaps they recalled the small parties of Lenape women who gathered seasonally to collect plants for baskets, mats, and medicines at traditional locations used for generations. Perchance some recalled the occasional Lenape men seeking wages or trade for work in their fields or Lenape women who came to work spinning flax alongside their Quaker sisters. It is hard to imagine any resident living in Chester County in 1797 who did not have some memory, personal or otherwise, of the Lenape people, who had lived in, worked in, and shared ownership of the place now called Pennsylvania. Hannah was a living reminder of another time, but not the present. For Chester County's residents the Lenape were a "vanishing race," and Hannah's novel appearance in town that day only reaffirmed their assumptions about former Indian neighbors.

Chester County's residents, like most citizens of the new United States, were enjoying the opportunities and bearing the uncertainties of a new nation in the last decade of the eighteenth century. In 1797 John Adams was the newly inaugurated president serving alongside vice president Thomas Jefferson: two men representing two political factions with very different visions of the nation's future. Political and economic leaders struggled to effect a balance between regulated growth and prosperity and the endless opportunities for economic exploitation and instability. The new nation had abundant resources and a youthful population ready to exploit those prospects. But the United States was also struggling to find compromise and common ideals among its diverse population. International affairs demanded that citizens of the new Republic take sides as England and France stood once again on the precipice of international warfare. Slavery was an issue that necessitated personal, local, and regional public commitment in support or opposition. Pennsylvania was the birthplace of the abolitionist movement, largely due to the Quakers' early stand against slavery. In 1787 the newly reorganized Pennsylvania Abolition Society, led by Benjamin Franklin, continued its consciousness-raising efforts and legal battles against slavery. Despite these efforts many farmers in Chester County continued to own slaves, and most likely Hannah crossed paths with her unfree neighbors as she traveled across the county attending to her daily work.[3]

Hannah saw many changes in the course of her life, but none was more transformative than the rapidly changing demographics of the region. In the census of 1790 nearly all of the 3.9 million Americans enumerated lived near the Atlantic coast. Hannah's homeland experienced the disruption created by the cosmopolitan efflorescence of Philadelphia, the largest American city at the end of the eighteenth century. In the aftermath of the Revolutionary War, the United States more than doubled its physical size, but the majority of those new lands were on the other side of the Appalachian Mountains, unsettled and in Indian possession. Hannah's kinsmen traveled from western Pennsylvania and Ohio to Philadelphia, regularly passing through their ancient homeland. Hannah probably heard their stories and wondered at one time or another if her family had made the right decision in staying behind. Delaware leaders in the western territories struggled to maintain old alliances with their ancient friends in Philadelphia, but other Indian alliances

The Examination of Hannah Freeman

with the British divided Hannah's people.[1] British soldiers continued to maintain forts west of the Appalachians, and many feared that Spain might close the port of New Orleans on the Mississippi River to American commerce. Domestic transportation and communication remained primitive, unreliable, and undeveloped, especially in the backcountry, where many of the great resources remained untapped. The American population was a rapidly increasing diverse population spread over an expansive terrain. The key to the nation's success rested not only in the management and governance of the settled areas but in acquiring and settling the new lands to the west, largely held by the Delawares and other indigenous nations who rightfully resisted American encroachment.[5]

Hannah Freeman was not a citizen of this new nation. American Indian peoples living in the territorial boundaries of the new United States were not included in the visionary objectives of the new American Constitution. "We the people" was an exclusive ideal that barred Hannah Freeman and other native peoples from the protections and privileges of the "empire of liberty." Native peoples were not citizens, and they were not directly represented in the government. They held a unique but inconstant status within the American political system. The legacy of the treaty negotiations inherited from western European nations recognized Indian tribes as sovereign nations with rights of occupation but made no effort to clarify the political or legal identity of individual Indian peoples within the United States. Their place and future within the new nation was another issue that divided the citizenry. Most agreed that Native nations should not continue to control the new territories in the West because they were unqualified, incapable of making the best use of nature's bounty. Most also agreed that the reason they did not have the right to enjoy their ancient homelands was because they were not "civilized enough." Some, like Thomas Jefferson, believed that the eventual civilization of the American Indian peoples was possible, but expediency demanded that those more altruistic efforts would have to take a back-seat to the more immediate demand of expansion and economic growth. Others saw the Indian peoples as unredeemable, believing that their conquest and eventual elimination by any means necessary was the only solution to their "savagery." No matter what Americans perceived as the solution to their "Indian problem," most shared an essential objective: control and settlement of Indian lands. Pennsylvania's citizens shared these sentiments. From their point of view, Hannah Freeman was an object of pity, a relic, and a curiosity. She was the living embodiment of the destiny awaiting those native peoples who refused to accept the inevitable wave of "progress" that swept her people to a distant and tragic end (or so they thought). For Pennsylvanians, Hannah Freeman was the "last of her kind."[6]

Pennsylvanians claimed a unique solution to the Indian problem rooted in its colonial founding. William Penn, the Quaker founder of the colony, early on established an Indian policy based on the religious principals of the Society of Friends. Penn and his Quaker followers were committed to establishing a colony based on religious tolerance, democratic principles, and a strict code of personal morality that denounced violence and advocated the innate quality of all human beings. As a pacifist, Penn sought to avoid the bloodshed experienced throughout the Atlantic seaboard as European settlers laid claim to lands that were not their own. Penn's method was to purchase lands from the leaders of indigenous settlements and then resell them to European settlers. While Penn's personal commitment to a peaceful acquisition of Indian lands in Pennsylvania was unique relative to other colonial policies, the objective was the same: dispossession. Penn acknowledged the innate equality of all humans on a spiritual level, but he undoubtedly believed that the Indians were less civilized than his fellow English settlers. Penn's political legacy was short lived; not long after his death in 1718, his heirs began to abandon the "holy experiment" for the more lucrative objectives of wealth and expansion.[7]

The Examination of Hannah Freeman

The legacy of William Penn's self-proclaimed benevolent colonialism led to both the legal and illegal acquisition of all Lenape lands in southeastern Pennsylvania by the time of Hannah's birth. Despite Penn's personal promise to the Brandywine Lenape that their land claims along the river would be honored as long as they continued to reside there, his followers continued to parcel and plot lands still occupied by the Lenape peoples. By the 1750s Quaker pacifism and political leadership lost favor in Pennsylvania. Quakers would never again wield any major political power in the colony, but their legacy of pacifism and their reputation as mediators provided them a new opportunity to remain politically active and influential in Pennsylvania. In 1795, as Hannah became more and more dependent on the kindness of her neighbors, the Philadelphia Yearly Meeting (the central organizational body of Pennsylvania's Quaker constituency) established the Committee for the Improvement and Civilization of the Indian Nations. The Society of Friends reclaimed some of its former political authority and carved out its place in the new American Republic. During the war-torn years of the French and Indian War and the subsequent American Revolution, Quaker pacifism created a shadow of doubt regarding the loyalties of Penn's founding families. Their renewed commitment to public service inspired a new trajectory for their organization as Quaker leadership offered to serve the colony and later the new nation as mediators in treaty negotiations and agents of civilization through their missionary efforts. As the eighteenth century came to a close, Pennsylvania's citizens, both Quaker and otherwise, offered their solutions to the Indian problem and celebrated the legacy of William Penn's "holy experiment." Hannah was invisible to local Quakers, who cast their eyes further west when they offered their solutions to the "Indian problem." Hannah's continued occupation of her lands along the Brandywine was little more than an inconvenience to those who knew her and understood the implications of her claims.[8]

Hannah Freeman's health began to decline in the 1790s. In Native tradition, an aging Lenape woman was a revered and respected member of her community. She could rely on her extended kin to provide the necessities she was unable to provide for herself. She would have been sought out as a teacher to the young women in the community and as an advisor to her kin. She would have been regarded as a culture keeper for her people and most likely would have taught ceremonial responsibilities to the younger generation. Her knowledge of medicine and plants would have made her an especially esteemed member of the community, and probably she would have had several young apprentices. But Hannah was far removed from those customs and the community that would have recognized her importance. Now she was largely surrounded by a very different social network, which most likely perceived her as something quite different from a wisdom keeper. To her neighbors Hannah was a destitute, sick Indian woman who deserved sympathy and kindness. But she was arrogant in her land claims and foolish in her refusal to abandon her cabin. Eventually she became an obligation they sought to be rid of.[9]

There were many neighbors who were involved in one way or another with Hannah's final years in both an official and personal capacity, but there were several families who played an especially significant part, among these the Barnards. Richard Barnard was a familiar face to Hannah Freeman. As one of the first families of Chester County, Barnard was a well-known figure in this tight-knit Quaker community. He owned property in several townships, including Newlin, where Hannah kept her home. He owned extensive and very productive farmland and was an industrious and generous man. Quakers in Chester County still recall a story about Barnard's deep commitment to his faith. He had an ongoing dispute with a neighbor, Isaac Baily, a less "devoted" Friend, over access to water from a creek that bordered their properties. After multiple attempts to resolve the dispute fairly had failed, Barnard settled into a brief despair regarding

The Examination of Hannah Freeman

the conflict. He sought solace in his faith, following an inner light that directed him to go to his neighbor and wash his feet. It is said that Barnard's act of humble contrition so moved Isaac Baily that he immediately took a shovel to the disputed dam in the waterway. The two were devoted friends from then on. Barnard was also a leader among his neighbors, donating his own property and labor to building a local schoolhouse that also functioned as a meeting place for the newly forming Marlborough Meeting. Richard Barnard was an exemplary member of the local community, and his generosity extended to Hannah Freeman. As early as 1775 Barnard recorded his deliveries of apples and hay to Hannah's house. Occasionally he sent other farmhands to deliver milled grain or cider water for her personal use. When Hannah went for seasonal work on other neighboring farms, it was Richard Barnard who picked her up and delivered her where she was needed. Richard Barnard's good neighborliness was obviously motivated by his religious beliefs, but his ties to Hannah ran much deeper.[10]

Barnard, like many of her benefactors, lived on land that Hannah claimed and occupied as a Lenape woman. She understood that land to be hers according to a treaty the Brandywine Lenapes had signed with William Penn at the beginning of the eighteenth century. Hannah, her family, and her kin lived on those lands according to their customs of land tenure. Nevertheless, the Lenape lands lying along the Brandywine River were surveyed and sold, occupied and used, taxed and inherited by multiple generations of Quaker settlers who chose to ignore the Brandywine Lenapes' land claims. The extended families of the Barnards, Marshalls, Harlans, and Brintons, like so many of their neighbors, silenced Lenape land claims not through warfare, not through forced removal, but by sheer will of their own convictions.[11] Quakers, like most citizens of the new Republic, believed in the superiority of Western civilization and the inevitable demise of Indian civilizations. The destiny of the Lenape people was writ large by William Penn's benevolent brand of colonialism. His kindness and generosity, his offer of brotherhood and peace to Pennsylvania's Indian peoples enabled the Quakers who lived on Hannah's ancestral homelands to justify their own actions.[12] For those families and those local community members, Hannah Freeman was not just one old, sick Indian woman: she was the last reminder, the last placeholder for the Brandywine Lenape peoples. The final years of Hannah's life in Chester County were destined to stand as a testimony to William Penn's peaceable kingdom and his benevolent colonialism. For local historians, Hannah Freeman's life exonerated William Penn, his heirs, his colony, and the Society of Friends for their role in dispossessing the Delaware peoples of their homelands. Hannah Freeman never willingly left her lands. Throughout the 1790s, Richard Barnard and many others came forward to look after her, but by the end of the decade, as her health declined, her benefactors took steps to break their personal ties to Hannah Freeman and finally secure their claims to the former Lenape lands.

Hannah Freeman's appearance at the Chester County courthouse on July 28, 1797, was not voluntary. Moses Marshall, Chester County's justice of the peace, officially summoned her to appear at the court.[13] Marshall was another highly regarded Chester County resident. In 1797 he held multiple roles in the community besides justice of the peace: doctor, businessman, yeoman, and an exemplary member of the Society of Friends. Marshall had trained as a physician in Wilmington, Delaware, and served a unique internship as a medic for local regiments during the American Revolution, caring for the wounded at the battle of Brandywine in 1777. After the war, Marshall's interest in medicine seemed to wane as he pursued other occupations, though he was called "Dr. Marshall" all of his life. For some years after the revolution, he served as secretary to his uncle Humphry Marshall, a local botanist of some repute. In this capacity Moses Marshall traveled with his uncle collecting plant specimens and handling the business end of their horticultural venture.

The Examination of Hannah Freeman

His travels took him close to the combustible border of the colonial backcountry, from which most Chester County residents were insulated. Moses helped his uncle plant, harvest, and catalogue a wide variety of North American plant, shrub, and tree specimens. His entrepreneurial acumen served him well as he and his uncle developed a brisk business for the exportation of plants to American and European clients including Benjamin Franklin, Thomas Jefferson, and famous British physician John Fothergill. Moses Marshall and his uncle Humphry lived together in West Bradford Township until his uncle's death in 1801.[14]

The lands Moses Marshall inherited from his uncle were part of the original lands that William Penn had sold to his grandfather Abraham Marshall in 1713. As the Marshall family expanded and thrived on the fertile floodplains of the Brandywine River, Hannah's people and their presence diminished. The English settlers built dams to harness power for lumber and grain mills, plowed and fenced fields, and raised cattle and pigs. The more they developed the area, the more they undermined the ability of Hannah's people to live on the land. Moses Marshall in particular benefited from this family legacy, inheriting large tracts of land, the original Marshall homestead, a gristmill, and a sawmill. He leased some of the land to tenant farmers, and as evidenced by his account books did a brisk business at both mills. The Marshall family made such a huge footprint in West Bradford Township that the area was known as Marshalltown until after the Civil War. The majority of the Brandywine Lenapes reluctantly abandoned their ancestral home along the river because Chester County settlers refused to honor the terms of William Penn's treaty with local Lenape bands.[15] Some Lenape families, however, like Hannah's, chose to stay, and the newer local residents had little option except to accommodate the original owners. The pacifist Quakers could not physically raise arms against their persistent Lenape neighbors, and they had failed to legally evict them from their lands. The Marshall family and their Quaker neighbors lived on contested lands, whether they openly acknowledged it or not. Throughout her lifetime Hannah, her extended family, and others like her remained as living reminders of betrayal. When Moses Marshall and Hannah Freeman met at the courthouse on July 28, 1797, they were not strangers. They shared a long history, and Hannah's final years were of great importance to all her Quaker neighbors.

On that summer day in 1797, Hannah Freeman found herself in strange and unfamiliar surroundings. Earlier in the day a Quaker neighbor, most likely Richard Barnard, arrived to take her to West Chester, the county seat. Barnard's appearance was no surprise. In recent years he and other neighbors had undertaken responsibility for Hannah's care. They delivered her from one neighbor's house to another, where she received room and board for weeks at a time. She suffered from rheumatoid arthritis that left her unable to walk long distances or to mount her horse to travel throughout the region, as had been her lifelong custom. Her Quaker neighbors, compelled by their spiritual tenets and perhaps by their consciousness of guilt, provided Hannah with the necessities of her daily life. Her health had failed so rapidly in recent years that her neighbors and benefactors scattered along the Brandywine River were compelled more than ever to provide care for their old Lenape neighbor. On this warm, muggy morning in late July, Hannah, with Barnard's help, climbed onto a horse-drawn sulky that carried her to a meeting of grave importance.

The journey from Newlin Township to West Chester took Hannah and her driver through an intimately familiar landscape that she called home. But much that rolled out before her view that day must have appeared greatly altered since her younger days. As the surrey bumped along the dusty, rutted roads she probably noticed new fences, farms, and dirt roads that dissected and divided her ancient homeland. The trip to West Chester probably took several hours, and to an elderly, arthritic woman, it would have seemed much longer. Her journey took her across the Brandywine River, the living core of the land her kin and community had held for centuries. We cannot know what Hannah Freeman thought or felt as she passed over the Wawasan that summer day, but we can begin to understand the scene that unraveled when Hannah arrived at her destination.[16]

At the end of the eighteenth century West Chester was little more than a crossroads in rural Chester County, known mostly as the location of the Turks Head Tavern. Hannah Freeman had little reason to be familiar with West Chester in 1797. It was not a major center of commerce and it was only in the nascent stages of becoming the county's political hub. The Turks Head Tavern was situated on a ridge between the Brandywine River and the more easterly Chester Creek. It had taken on limited significance with the development of the east-west Philadelphia Pike, laid out in 1735, and the north-south Wilmington Road. Both roads connected Philadelphia and the Delaware Bay to Lancaster, Pennsylvania's backcountry center of commerce. But until the 1780s the intersection offered travelers, traders, Indians, and soldiers nothing more than a tavern, a blacksmith, and local wares sold by peddlers and farmers. It was a rough-hewn beginning for a town described in 2001 as "one of the world's most perfect small towns."[17] Nineteenth-century regional historians J. Smith Futhey and Gilbert Cope complained that the town was laid out "with utter disregard of symmetry" relative to the better conceived and planned Philadelphia twenty-four miles to the east.[18]

Just a few short years before Hannah Freeman journeyed to West Chester in 1797, growth and prosperity had placed new demands on this backwater community. During the second half of the eighteenth century, Chester County ranked as the third-wealthiest county in Pennsylvania, behind Philadelphia and Lancaster, due largely to its agricultural productivity. Most of the county's commerce was directed toward Philadelphia to the east, but its political and legal business lay to the southernmost edge of the county in Chester. Therefore, prosperous Chester County residents took steps to relocate the county seat to a more central location and, after some minor but colorful protests, succeeded. In 1784 the Pennsylvania legislature legitimized this move, allowing county residents to initiate changes that injected the necessary commercial fuel into the local economy.

The first order of business was the identification and naming of the physical boundaries of the new community. These actions alone, whether one recognized them as legitimate or not, had the effect of erasing prior claims to the land in the new Republic. Renaming, drawing boundary lines, and mapping rivers, towns, and other landscape features enabled the new settlers to efface the region's ancient indigenous identity and begin the construction of a wholly new one. West Chester, an unimaginative choice for the new county seat, solidified its elevated role by claiming continuity with the previous seat of political authority in Chester at the same time as it obscured its less dignified origins as nothing more than the site of a colorfully named tavern for wayfarers. The town, the county, and the river and its tributaries bore no resemblance or connections to its centuries-old Lenape heritage. The only evidence of the previous legacy rested in the memories of local residents, the remnants of some structures, and the persistent Native residents who never left.

Richard Barnard delivered Hannah to the recently completed courthouse situated near the northwest corner of High Street (north-south route) and Gay Street (east-west route). As she carefully stepped down onto the dirt road, she was naturally compelled to look at her surroundings. In the thirteen short years since its elevation to county seat, the town showed evidence of its rapid transformation from a dusty backwater. In her immediate view was the county courthouse, built in 1786, her destination that day. The hurriedly constructed, clapboard-covered two-story building was described by one town founder as "shabby." Nevertheless, it was the tallest structure in town and the weathervane-topped cupola must have drawn Hannah's attention. As she looked up and down the streets, the panorama in-

The Examination of Hannah Freeman

cluded no fewer than four new hotels built to serve the business-
es and visitors drawn to the county seat. Looking south from the
town center, she may have passed the small houses under construction on lots recently parceled from the old Hoopes farm.
On any given day one could have heard the pounding of nails
and smelled the fresh lumber brought in from the surrounding
sawmills. West Chester was ready to enter the nineteenth century, showing all the signs of economic prosperity and growth
that Pennsylvania's Quaker founder William Penn had imagined for his colony. For Hannah Freeman the town, the construction, and the hustle-bustle of the county seat probably represented something very different.[19]

Hannah Freeman appeared before Moses Marshall not as a
neighbor but in response to an official summons to determine
her future status as a pauper in Chester County. Marshall had
a dual role that day. He was the acting justice of the peace and
also the overseer of the poor for a district that included East Fal-
lowfield, Pennsbury, East Bradford, and West Bradford townships and most important Newlin Township, the site of Hannah's
home. Marshall's official responsibility was to assess Hannah's
legal residency and determine which township was financially
responsible for her care. Chester County was on the verge of a
transition to a more institutionalized form of care for the poor,
and Hannah Freeman was among those who stood to "benefit"
from this modernization. Despite his lifelong familiarity with
Hannah and his family's full awareness of the generations-old
land dispute, Moses Marshall summoned his full authority as
overseer of the poor and justice of the peace as he asked Hannah Freeman to prove her residency in Newlin Township. We
cannot know how this interview appeared to Hannah that day.
Did Richard Barnard or Moses Marshall explain the meaning
of the proceedings to her? Did Hannah question their unusual
behavior or demand an explanation? More than one neighbor
described Hannah as a strong-willed woman, almost arrogant
in her demeanor. Did she stand tall that day, look Marshall in

the eye, and demand an explanation for all his questions? Or did she resist his questions with silences? We cannot know. But we do know that Moses Marshall, pen in hand, proceeded to record a brief history of Hannah Freeman's life in the region based on her testimony. His objective was to establish and date her residence and pattern of work. Hannah's objective was to remember her life, her family, her work, and her land.

Hannah, a tall, lean Lenape woman, stood before Marshall and remembered that "she was born in a cabin on William Webb's place." She named the places she had lived, where she had worked, and what she was paid. The interview, whether it proceeded as a series of questions or as a request that she tell her own story, would have evoked some curiosity and doubt on her part. Hannah grew up in the Brandywine Lenapes' oral tradition, in which a family history was a living thing of great value. She understood the importance of the written word and understood she was "going on the record." The narrative Marshall recorded shows a tension between what he valued and needed to record and what Hannah Freeman valued and chose to remember.

This tension is particularly evident when Hannah explains why she did not continue to stay with her closest living relative Nanny, even after the deaths of her grandmother and mother. As Hannah explains, "she then went to her Aunt Nanny at Concord but having forgot to talk Indian and not liking their manner of living so well as white peoples she came to Kennett & lived at Wm Webbs." Taken at face value, her statement suggests that Hannah had strong feelings about remaining close to her own home near the Brandywine River and maintaining her independence, the very issue that was being called into question at the deposition that day.

But what other interpretations does this statement suggest? Marshall's objective is to create a record that validates her residency, but it is complicated by the fact that she is not just any resident in the county. Legally, she is a nonperson, not a citizen or a taxpayer. Chester County's residents offered no legal place for Indians living in their county. Marshall might simply have interpreted her statement as some proof of her assimilation into white culture, the foundation of late nineteenth-century Quaker missionary ideology, thus deserving of their benevolence. It is what he needed to know and her statement proved useful to fulfilling his task as the justice of the peace. For Marshall it was all about residency, corroborating dates, and employment record. Those were the details he legally needed to demonstrate her dependency and assign financial responsibility to taxpayers.

We cannot leave her statement without making some effort to retrieve Hannah's voice in the passage, whether or not the words were of her own choosing. Again, simply stated: she did not want to live with her elderly aunt in Concord. Hannah claims she almost "forgot to talk Indian," which is plausible considering that she interacted on a daily basis with non-Delaware speakers and as she grew older the opportunities to interact with other Delawares were nearly absent. But her claims to language attrition might also indicate that she understood exactly what Marshall needed to know. Language, perhaps more than any other factor, provides the most dynamic and personal link to one's culture. It is hard to imagine that Hannah forgot the language of her prayers, ceremonies, and songs—the very living link to her people and her place in the Brandywine valley. She was facing Marshall in an unusual circumstance. The more he could associate her with white culture and the more she could distance herself from the Delaware "way of living," the better her chance of success. For Marshall her identity as a Lenape woman was tethered to external factors he recognized: how she dressed, spoke, and interacted in the community. What he did not understand was that Hannah's identity as a Lenape woman was situated in her heart and mind. It is that identity she consistently expressed all her life.

Hannah's narrative is interjected with memories of her mother, father, and extended family. She recalled personal loss—"her

Granny died about the Schuylkill, her Aunt Betty at Middleton and her mother at Centre"—as well as the violence and uncertainty in her life when "the Indians were not allowed to plant corn anymore" and the critical point when "her father went to Shamokin and never returned."[20] Marshall undoubtedly edited Hannah's responses and prompted her with questions in order to create the linear, formulaic narrative required for this official process. He wrote the transcription in ink, but the document shows how he broke off, restarted, scored through some words he had written and added others as her testimony continued. Marshall omitted much that Hannah Freeman told him, but the official "Examination of Indian Hannah" ultimately fulfilled the county's needs by proving that she was a resident of Newlin Township. Poor taxes paid by Newlin's property owners would underwrite the expense of Hannah's care.

It is unlikely that Hannah Freeman fully understood the importance of her deposition that day, but we can be certain that Moses Marshall did. Chester County, like many regional governments of the new Republic, was transitioning to a more economically efficient way of handling the burgeoning numbers of the poor and homeless in the rural and urban communities of the former thirteen colonies. Demographic growth and postwar recovery in Chester County placed new demands on the older system of charity, which relied heavily on outrelief, that is, assistance given to people living outside institutions. Public assistance came in the form of cash payments, food, housing, medical care, and a myriad of other provisions. As early as 1718 Chester County passed laws that attempted to regulate charity for the poor and provide accounting of their outrelief to local taxpayers. Along with the power to levy an adequate poor tax on the residents, the overseers arbitrated disputes regarding the legal residence of the paupers. Overseers investigated cases between townships when paupers' claims to residency were rejected. When named townships refused responsibility for individual claims, the county's Court of Quarter Sessions made the

The Examination of Hannah Freeman

final determination. Paupers who qualified for outrelief were required by law to wear on the right shoulder of their clothing the letter *P* and the first letter of their township name, cut from red or blue cloth, in "an open and visible manner." Any person who refused or neglected to wear the letters was subject to punishment that could include loss of relief, imprisonment, whipping, or bound labor.[21]

Hannah Freeman was a recipient of unofficial community charity prior to her deposition in 1797. By that time she was no longer living in her own home but staying permanently with neighbors. Those who looked after Hannah Freeman did not seek reimbursement for their expenses through any official channels. Until 1797 they were willing to keep Hannah's support off the record. It is hard to imagine that her neighbors wanted or expected Hannah to wear the red or blue letter *P*. It is even more implausible to imagine that Hannah would have agreed to do so. Hannah had been a self-sufficient woman all of her life. Her need for local charity was directly related to her declining health and advancing age. She does not appear on any official records as a pauper prior to her examination in 1797. By all accounts, Hannah's Quaker neighbors cared for her as they would an elderly family member or a member of their religious community. They were guided by their community's moral principles, and the informal charitable support they offered Hannah is not surprising. But in 1797 Hannah's appearance before Moses Marshall at the Chester County courthouse marked an abrupt change in her status. Her testimony ultimately gave him the legal authority to commit Hannah to the Chester County poorhouse.[22]

In March 1798 thirty-four Quaker men gathered together at the home of Hannah's good friend and neighbor Richard Barnard to enter into a formal contract in which they agreed to provide "more permanent" care for Hannah Freeman. In less than a year after the "examination" Hannah's care within her community had shifted from an informal neighborly understanding, not unlike one she might have enjoyed in a Lenape town, to a formal contracted agreement that required depositions, signatures, trustees, and a treasurer. Hannah may or may not have been aware of this shift, but those who knew her understood the significance of their obligations and the need to alter their relationship with the old Indian woman who lived down the road. The signatories gathered at Richard Barnard's house acknowledged that "Indian Hannah" was ill and unable to care for herself "as was her usual custom" because she was "afflicted with rheumatism." Barnard's informal contract, titled "Kindness Extended," paints a brief but detailed portrait of his neighbor, stating that her rheumatism prevented her from supporting herself because she could no longer travel from place to place on horseback to earn her living, as she was "accustomed to." Barnard provided a rare glimpse of an independent woman who never abandoned her Lenape way of life but instead continued to live "in a manner suited to her way of living." From his perspective, Hannah's way of life was evidence of her failure to assimilate into the dominant English way of living. The thirty-four Quaker men who read and affirmed the contract would never have considered that perhaps it was Hannah who, quietly and consistently, had compelled her neighbors to adapt to her, accepting her Lenape way of life and her persistent occupation of the ancient homelands.[23]

It is significant that Barnard declares in the contract that Hannah Freeman is an "ancient woman of the Delaware tribe" and "the only person of that description left amongst us." It is curious that Barnard and those assembled to formally acknowledge their role as her benefactors declared Hannah the "last of her kind." They knew she was not. At the end of the eighteenth century there were Indian people living throughout the Pennsylvania, New Jersey, and Delaware regions. Many were living their lives independent of formal tribal communities, which had relocated beyond the Appalachian Mountains. As late as 1909 a local Chester County newspaper reported the death in

The Examination of Hannah Freeman

Newlin Township of Lydia Sharp, the "last of the Lenni Lenape tribe."[24] Descendants of the Lenapes and other Native communities still live throughout the region, such as the Nanticoke-Lenape community in New Jersey within fifty miles of West Chester. Considering this evidence, the declaration that Hannah Freeman "was the only person of that description left amongst us" takes on new meaning. Subsequent generations of Pennsylvanians declared Hannah Freeman "the last of her kind," telling and retelling the story as proof that the Quakers in Pennsylvania continued to fulfill William Penn's benevolent Indian policy. Within a generation after her death "Indian Hannah" became a local legend, an artifact offered as evidence of the "peaceable kingdom."

If we put aside the impact of this declaration on later generations of Pennsylvanians and return to what Barnard and his fellow signers intended by this document, it becomes clear that caring for Hannah Freeman in her final years was important to her neighbors. The contract provides an organizational structure that imitates the county's official provisions for the poor. Hannah's neighbors appointed two trustees to oversee the "disposal" of the collected resources and provide "full accounts of what they have received." The trustees were to be appointed every year, and the treasurer could not pay out any funds without the trustees' written consent. The resources were to be provided either by those who subscribed "to keep her" by offering Hannah room and board for specific lengths of time or those who signed on to "pay money." Twenty-one subscribed to "pay money" annually for Hannah's support and the remainder offered room and board. Many names on that list appear and reappear in relationship to Hannah: Barnard, Marshall, Harlan, Hayes, and Pierce, the family names of her closest neighbors and lifelong friends. The contract also provides funds to be used for burial expenses at the time of her death, stipulating that any remaining funds will be returned to those in "proportion to what they have advanced" for her yearly care. So the question remains:

Why were Hannah Freeman's neighbors compelled to create a formal, albeit private, contractual arrangement for her relief? Why did they substitute their previous informal care with this bureaucratically inspired legal contract?

One cannot read the contract without getting a sense of their genuine compassion and the obligation they felt to "provide" for Hannah Freeman, but this does not explain why they declared that compassion in such precise monetary terms. When this document is considered along with the "Examination of Hannah Freeman" composed the previous summer, it suggests that those involved needed to have their relationship with Hannah Freeman officially documented, even though the "Kindness Extended" was never publicly exhibited or used. While the "Examination of Hannah Freeman" served to determine which township was liable for her support under the county's poor tax laws, the "Kindness Extended" remained a private document preserved in the Barnard family Bible for generations. However, considering other changes taking place in Chester County relative to the care for the poor will shed light on her neighbors' motivations.

A few short months after Hannah's deposition at the courthouse in the summer of 1797 and before the private gathering at Richard Barnard's in the spring of 1798, Chester County was actively taking steps to provide for the needs of the burgeoning poor by moving away from outrelief to the institutionalization of the poor. Before the American Revolution, the combination of private charity and local outrelief was an adequate solution to the problem. But increased immigration and the new mobility of the laboring poor left many townships and local charities hard pressed to provide for those in need, and the escalation in the number of disputes between overseers of the poor reflect these changes. The primary objective of new poor laws was to prevent nonresident indigents from gaining legal access to local relief. Moses Marshall, as justice of the peace for Chester County, witnessed the rising number of disputes and understood

The Examination of Hannah Freeman

2. Chester County Alms House, Newlin. (Photograph by J. Max Mueller.
Courtesy of the Chester County Historical Society, West Chester,
Pennsylvania)

that local demands were outpacing official resources. Previous
recipients of the taxpayers' benevolence were the widowed, or-
phaned, elderly, and disabled. The majority were women. Hannah's circumstances were not unusual in an eighteenth-century
agrarian-based economy, and local residents provided those in
need with room and board in exchange for work, with the understanding that they could turn to the county coffers to offset
any expenses related to their charity. The new paupers were different, including able-bodied men and women who were either
unemployed or earning an income inadequate to support their
families. They moved from township to township, seeking work
and relief, and increasing tax revenues to support this cost was
an unwelcome solution for county taxpayers.[25]

In February 1798 the Chester County General Assembly passed
an act to provide funds for the building and maintenance of a
county poorhouse. Moses Marshall was one of nine men elected
as initial poorhouse commissioners, instructed to plan the construction of the poorhouse and project the budget. (Six poorhouse directors were to be elected every two years to take on the

permanent duties of administering the poorhouse; John Marshall, Moses's son, was elected to that office in 1800, the year the poorhouse opened its doors.) The directors' first priority was to purchase land. Just several months after Hannah's thirty-four benefactors met at Richard Barnard's home to sign the "Kindness Extended," Stephen Harlan, one of them, invited the poorhouse directors to view his property, and they swiftly agreed to purchase a portion of the Harlan farm. Harlan's property, like Moses Marshall's, had belonged to the Brandywine Lenape and was one of the parcels sold by Nathaniel Newlin earlier in the century. Deborah and Stephen Harlan were more than local landowners; they were Hannah's neighbors and friends. The land offered by the Harlans for the Chester County poorhouse was land that Hannah Freeman had a legal claim to. There is no suggestion that Hannah's historical claim was remembered or considered in this transaction, but it is hard to imagine that the irony of the situation completely escaped all of the participants that day. Stephen Harlan could not sell unencumbered land. Did Hannah's failing health and newly emerging status as a county pauper signal that she no longer had any legal claim to those lands? It may even explain why her benefactors insisted on declaring Hannah Freeman the "the only person of that description [Lenape] left amongst us." It fulfilled William Penn's original treaty stipulation that the lands belonged to her people until the last one had abandoned them.[26]

The land sale did not go completely uncontested. Curiously, Deborah Harlan, Stephen's wife, is on record as initially refusing to agree to this sale. Her refusal is unexplained, but it was four months before Deborah Harlan agreed to the sale of the property, in March of 1799, when she accepted a "present of thirty dollars" for her signature. Why did Deborah Harlan resist signing the sale? We can be certain that she was not attempting to increase the price of the property, because the purchase price is unchanged except for her "gift." Did she object because she understood the history of the property and knew that her family did not have the right to sell what was not legally theirs? Was she expressing an allegiance or loyalty to Hannah Freeman, a friend who sat by the Harlans' fire many nights, tended their children, worked on their farm? Or was she merely resisting the relocation of hundreds of indigent inmates to her own neighborhood? While Deborah Harlan's motivations are uncertain, we do know that she succeeded in delaying the construction of the poorhouse during that period.[27]

Despite Deborah Harlan's brief obstruction, the construction of the poorhouse began in earnest in March of 1799 and was completed to everyone's satisfaction by November 1800. The Chester County poorhouse was built according to specifications obtained by the directors during their visit to the neighboring New Castle in Wilmington, Delaware. The institutions shared an external and internal esthetic. Outward projections of the residents' Christian morality, the poorhouses represented the good intentions of the citizens in regard to their responsibilities for their unfortunate neighbors. Poorhouses were meant to be a temporary solution. They were working farms, and all inmates who were able were expected to be part of the workforce. The building was a two-story, brick-faced structure with a colonnaded front veranda that outwardly exhibited both the efficiency and frugality of the Quaker taxpayers whose extensive properties surrounded the almshouse. While the exterior of the poorhouse fit easily into the prosperous landscape of well-tended working farms, the interior reflected something quite different.[28]

Chester County poorhouse was designed to hold up to two hundred inmates. The first floor opened into an interior designed as a dormitory and provided space for administration, the kitchen, and common eating areas, but the second floor erased any association with the ambience or warmth of local farmhouses. The second floor was organized as a dormitory, a series of plain sleeping rooms for multiple occupants. The rooms were sparsely furnished with beds and an occasional chair. Inmates were seldom allowed to bring personal items to the poorhouses, if they had any. The time spent as an inmate was meant to teach a lesson about the gravity of their condition. Hard work, not comfort, was understood as the solution. Caretakers provided a minimal diet, and the inmates' daily existence revolved around mealtimes and tasks assigned by the caretakers.

From the orderly collection of poor tax to the construction of an efficient poorhouse, Chester County's leaders and residents were proud of their modern and humanitarian response to the growing demands of the county's poorer citizens. Moses Marshall, Stephen Harlan, Richard Barnard, and all of the benefactors who signed the "Kindness Extended" in 1798 facilitated the creation of the poorhouse on Hannah's ancestral homelands. Moses Marshall's questions about her life, Richard Barnard's declaration that Hannah Freeman was the "last of her kind," and the commitment of her neighbors to provide for her in her final years were all public, formal acts that sealed Hannah Freeman's fate.

On November 12, 1800, Hannah Freeman sat next to the large open hearth, a favorite place in her neighbor's home. On this chilly morning in November the fire must have been especially comforting for her stiff arthritic joints. Perhaps she sat at the fire talking to the children or doing some task for the family. Perhaps she was preparing to say good-bye, knowing that in a short time another neighbor would arrive to deliver her to a new destination. The routine move from one neighbor to another was an all too familiar experience for Hannah by this time. Over the last year she had spent most of her time with Richard Barnard's family but had also stayed for fairly long periods with the Marshalls and Harlans. But this day her destination was to be different. On this day Caleb Marshall and Joshua Buffington, acting as Newlin County's overseers of the poor, arrived to deliver Hannah Freeman to the Chester County poorhouse a few short miles away. We cannot know whether Hannah was prepared for this change or if she understood where she was going,

The Examination of Hannah Freeman

but we can imagine that the change in her care was harsh and abrupt. On November 12, 1800, five of the six commissioners of the poor received inmates from nineteen townships, including Newlin. Hannah Freeman is one of the first inmates recorded in the admissions book. Over two days the directors received ninety-four inmates from most of the county's townships. Before leaving the poorhouse to the care of its supervisor, one final act required the immediate attention of the commissioners. On November 13 the directors decided on a fixed location for a graveyard. Of the ninety-four inmates, seven were elderly. The directors were a practical group of administrators. They believed Hannah would never leave the poorhouse.[29]

It is hard to imagine what Hannah Freeman was thinking or feeling that day as she was escorted to one of the second-floor dormitory rooms. Was Hannah treated like the other inmates, or did her neighbors and friends provide for some exceptions or concessions for her care? Was she allowed to bring personal things that were important to her—ceremonial objects, family heirlooms, items she held close as reminders of her people, her family? Later residents of Chester County occasionally made public declarations about having something that used to belong to the "last of the Lenape": silver spoons, baskets, beadwork. We can speculate that those who signed the "Kindness Extended" took charge of Hannah's material possessions, disposing of them as they saw fit. Perhaps the few possessions they believed held any value were sold or claimed by those who had contributed to her care. Possibly her cabin was dismantled or abandoned to the elements and her furniture, dishes, tools, and animals were divided among her benefactors as well. We can be certain that when Hannah Freeman walked across the front veranda of the poorhouse and climbed the stairs to her new "home," little of her former life came with her except her memories and her identity as a Lenape woman. Her recollections and family history, her prayers and songs cannot be undervalued. They sustained her through a lifetime of living Lenape in a colonial world. We can only imagine what Hannah thought as she looked out from her room and gazed across her homelands. Perhaps she found peace in remembering the well-tended gardens of her mothers and grandmothers, or the river running thick with shad. Just maybe Hannah Freeman understood something that her neighbors never did: the Lenapes are still here. They never went away.

CHAPTER TWO

All Our Grandmothers

It is not hard to imagine that Hannah Freeman's grandmother might have stood on the same hill where the Chester County poorhouse was built and looked out on a landscape that would be much changed within two generations. The hilltop location offered a panoramic view of the lands claimed by the Brandywine Lenapes, the rolling hills and valleys that Hannah's family called home. We can imagine a cold spring morning, the ground hard with frost. She may have stood on the hilltop and offered a traditional prayer to the rising of the sun in the east and looked to the stars in the sky still visible in the predawn darkness. With her prayers finished, she may have looked up to name the stars in the sky. Like all the Lenape women before her, she was adept at reading the night sky, using the locations of the constellations and the moon to determine the time to plant, harvest, and prepare the medicines that kept her people well.[1] She could name them all and remembered the stories they held. It was the season when days grew longer and winter was behind her. This full moon was especially significant because it signaled the beginning of the planting season. On this day her family and kin would gather together and prepare a special meal, laughing, sharing stories, and remembering their ancestors. They would bring fish from the river and celebrate in anticipation of a good spring and summer that would provide an abundance of food for her people. Together they would renew the relationship with their ancestors and the land they had known since the time before time. Nothing could have prepared

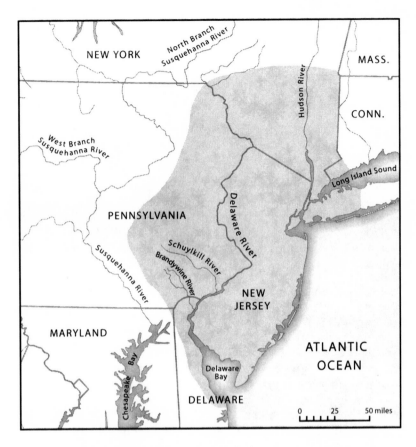

Map 1. Historic occupation of the Lenapes at contact.

them for the changes in their immediate future. Neither their wisest women nor their most respected leaders could have foreseen the world that Hannah Freeman would know.

Far from the Brandywine River, far from any lands the Lenape knew, King Charles II signed a royal proclamation that would forever alter the lives of the Lenapes in Pennsylvania. As the Brandywine Lenapes celebrated the beginning of spring, William Penn was celebrating the culmination of his greatest endeavor. On March 5, 1681, King Charles II granted Penn the sole proprietorship of a colony he named Pennsylvania. The grant conferred on William Penn full title to forty-five thousand square miles of land, bordered on the east by the Delaware River, to the south by Lord Baltimore's Maryland colony, and to the north the colony belonging to the king's brother the Duke of York. The western boundaries of Penn's new colony were unknown—but claimed nonetheless. Pennsylvania, the twelfth of the thirteen original colonies, was remarkable on several counts. By 1680 the king and his ministers were tightening their control of their North American colonies. Continued threats from French expansion to the north and west and Indian wars in New England and the Chesapeake threatened the economic and political stability of the king's lands in North America and also had a negative impact on the Crown's wealth. Some of the colonies were governed by corporate partnerships, others by a lord proprietor or a group of proprietors, and to each was granted varying degrees of self-governance to local assemblies and governors. The king's authority directly governed only one colony, Virginia. The grant for the Pennsylvania colony came at a time when the Crown sought to limit local colonial authority and impose restrictions and regulations on colonial proprietors and legislative bodies. Despite these trends, William Penn's petition, submitted in May of 1680, took an unprecedented ten short months to pass through the Lords of Trade and the Privy Council. The king granted Penn sole proprietorship and made him the "true and absolute ruler" of his own colony with authority to create a government, enact and implement laws, and raise an army if needed.[2] Of course, King Charles II had reason to move quickly and sympathetically in regard to Penn's petition. William Penn's father, the late admiral Sir William Penn, had served in the king's navy and supported the restoration of Charles II in 1660. Indebted to the Penn family for both their loyalty and their financial support (Penn's father supplied the Royal Navy with food and was never compensated), the king made this land grant to discharge his royal debt, paving the way for the settlement of the mid-Atlantic lands that were understood to be "altogether Indian."[3]

The charter was doubly remarkable due to the character of the colony's new proprietor. William Penn was a member of the Society of Friends, commonly known as Quakers. The young Penn, unlike his father and the king, was not a member of the Church of England, the only state-sanctioned religion at that time. Penn's youthful rebelliousness against established authorities found its most committed expression in his conversion to the Quaker religion. The Society of Friends, founded by George Fox in mid-seventeenth-century England, had emerged during a time of religious turmoil in Europe. Quakers rejected the clergy as intermediaries between the believer and God. They believed that God communicated directly with each person who received the "inner light," and they eschewed the rituals and doctrines of most Christian traditions. For William Penn and his fellow Friends, a life of simplicity, peace, prosperity, and equality were the guiding objectives. Along with rejecting ordained clergy, sacraments, and the infallibility of the Bible, Quakers also challenged long-accepted social customs of English culture. They were pacifists in a world where war was an assumed way of life, and they rejected the authority of their social superiors. Quakers refused to bow before kings, swear oaths in court, or even take off their hats in the company of those who held social or political ranks above them. William Penn's decision to join the Society of Friends in 1667 was a radical departure from his elite

All Our Grandmothers

heritage that landed him in prison on four different occasions and permanently ruptured his relationship with his father the admiral. It is hard to imagine a more unlikely candidate for a colonial proprietorship in the 1680s than William Penn: whether King Charles's motivation was to rid himself of the old debt or of the Quaker nuisance in England, the outcome was the same. In August 1682 William Penn set sail for his new colony, named for his father: Pennsylvania.

William Penn sailed up the Delaware River on October 26, 1682, in his aptly named ship, *Welcome*. His first landing, at present-day Newcastle, Delaware, saw the performance of one of many acts of legendary ceremony faithfully recalled by chroniclers of the colony's history. Penn presented his deed to the English commissioners, who acknowledged the legality of the documents. In a feudal ceremony they presented the key to the fort, which Penn used to first lock the gate and then reopen it, demonstrating his command of the territory. In turn, the commissioners enacted an ancient custom, presenting Penn with a symbolic piece of sod, a twig, and a bowl of river water, demonstrating their acceptance of his authority and their allegiance to the new government. The ship then continued its journey north, finally landing at the Swedish settlement of Upland, where Penn disembarked. The festivities continued, and "Dutch, Swedes, and English . . . received and entertained him with great expressions of joy." Penn addressed the audience, explained his plan for government, and assured the people of their "spiritual and temporal rights," requiring from them only "sobriety and loving neighborhood."[1] The symbolic performances surrounding Penn's arrival and his first claim to the colony are rife with irony, considering that the true proprietors of the extensive lands Penn's charter claimed were not present to greet him in the official ceremonies of the day. We do not know if any Lenapes watched Penn's ship the *Welcome* sail up the Delaware River and land at Newcastle or whether Lenape canoes joined the procession as the ship tacked north to its final landing in

Upland. It is easy to imagine that there were Lenape onlookers that day, either on the shores, in the towns, or following the *Welcome* on the water. A European ship was not an unfamiliar sight to Lenapes; it was understood as an opportunity for the trade and exchange they were well accustomed to.

In the late seventeenth century Hannah Freeman's kin living in southeastern Pennsylvania were well acquainted with European settlers. The Lenapes, extraordinary farmers, lived on some of the most fertile soils in eastern North America, known today as the Piedmont. The rivers and creeks that passed through their country deposited fertile soils that Hannah's ancestors farmed for thousands of years. Modern geographers suggest that southeastern Pennsylvania was "very close to being ideal" for farming and one of "the most productive bits of territory" on the continent, blessed with a good climate and rainfall. The Lenapes cultivated an abundance of agricultural crops that European settlers depended upon for their survival in the first decades after their landings on the Atlantic coast.[5] Dutch, Swedish, and English colonists sequentially settled on Lenape lands throughout the seventeenth century. Dutch settler Adriaen van der Donck marveled at the abundance and diversity of the crops: the squash was a "pleasing fruit" grown in abundance, the beans "grow in great variety," their growth "lush and profuse." Robert Juet, sailing for Henry Hudson in 1609, eagerly remarked that the Lenapes "have a great store of Maiz" and appeared willing not only to trade but also to share with the visiting strangers. When the sailors ventured onto land, the Lenapes greeted them with gifts of tobacco and also showed them where they could find currants and acorns, both portable food sources. In turn, Lenape men, women, and children boarded the ship with gifts for the captain. Juet, with an eye for marketable commodities, observed that the Lenapes were dressed in "Skinnes of divers sorts and good Furres."[6]

The Lenapes' agricultural expertise satisfied the needs of hungry European colonists, who were not immediately success-

All Our Grandmothers

ful cultivating their own crops. Supply ships from Europe were unreliable, and the Lenapes were more than willing to rise to the economic opportunity. Other observers noted that the Lenapes were known not just for the quality of the foodstuffs they traded, but also for the quantity of fields they cultivated. Within decades they cornered the local market by assessing colonial needs and building their tradable stores to meet the settlers' demands. Lenape trade goods included deer, elk, and bear meat, fresh fish of "all kinds," wild turkeys, grouse, fruits and nuts including apples, peaches, watermelons, chestnuts and walnuts, and wild hops used to make beer, which especially pleased the Dutch and Swedish consumers. The marketable goods the Lenapes brought to trade and sell were not limited to food items. Men and women traded over fifteen different kinds of animal skins. They were also expert painters and craftspeople. Lenape women made skin bags of different sizes, painted in detail using a variety of colors extracted from local mineral and plant sources. They sold woven mats, baskets, and quilts made of local bulrushes and rattlesnake grass found along the rivers and marshlands. They adorned their work with painted feathers, shells, and bones; all were in great demand by the colonists.[7] Few examples of their work exist today, but a hint of their artistry can be seen in the tattoo designs displayed on the bodies of Lenape men and women recorded by curious Europeans in their earliest encounters.[8]

In exchange for food and other resources, the Lenapes acquired European clothing, guns, and a variety of tools that made their lives easier. Hannah's grandmother probably used European sewing needles to attach wampum shells onto the belts exchanged in ceremonies and communication. Lenape women used pewter spoons to serve stews from brass kettles. Scissors, sugar, hoes, and mirrors were all part of the exchange between Lenapes living along the Brandywine River and their Dutch, Swedish, and English neighbors. By the time William Penn arrived in Pennsylvania, Lenape women wore knee-length skirts made from the cloth acquired in trade, although they also wore leggings and moccasins made from traditional textiles. They decorated their clothing with bells made from thimbles and painted their faces in ancient designs using plant and mineral pigments. Lenape women were selective regarding which European goods they chose to incorporate into their own kitchens and homes as well as how to use the new items. Brass kettles were much preferred to any clay-based cooking pot, but there was not an English substitute for the wooden mortars and pestles made from a tree stump to grind corn into the fine meal used to make their traditional breads. Lenape women and men braided local hemp and other plant fibers to make both strong ropes and fine fishing nets, which settlers began to incorporate into their own everyday lives. Hannah's grandmothers and the women of that generation grew up in a world of lively exchange and adaptations that traveled back and forth between their homes and those of the European settlers.[9]

Unfortunately, not all of the exchanges between Hannah's kin and the European settlers were desirable ones. The Lenapes, like other indigenous Americans, experienced wave after wave of epidemic diseases introduced by contact with European colonists. It is hard to estimate how many Lenapes died from the killer diseases of smallpox, measles, and the multiple other pathogens introduced with European contact, but by the seventeenth century the Lenapes living in the river valleys of southeastern Pennsylvania were devastated by the effects. In 1663 and 1677 colonists recorded four separate epidemics that spread through Lenape communities. Unlike many other epidemic diseases, which killed the most vulnerable members of the population, the young and old, smallpox took the lives of mothers and fathers, husbands and wives, farmers and fishers of the community. In the late 1600s a German minister who lived in Pennsylvania commented that "a great many savages have died, even since I came here, so that there are hardly more than a fourth part of their number existing that were to be seen when I came to the country ten years ago." Another settler, Gabriel Thomas, claimed that "two of them die for every one Christian that comes here."[10] It is hard to imagine how that level of loss in a community impacted families, towns, and day-to-day living, which required a strong and healthy populace. Crops rotted in the fields, fishnets remained unrepaired, and ceremonies went unfulfilled as the rural settlements succumbed to smallpox, influenza, and measles. Sometimes the diseases destroyed communities and families beyond healing. Fortunately, although Hannah's grandmothers and grandfathers probably lost friends and family to the dreaded diseases, the Brandywine River community recovered from its losses and continued to thrive.

Despite the material changes that were a part of everyday life for the Lenapes in southeastern Pennsylvania in the late seventeenth century, the Brandywine villages still enjoyed a relative separation from English settlers, who were purchasing lands from the Lenapes living closer to the Delaware River. The Brandywine and its tributary streams remained unencumbered by English dams and there were no Quaker farmers fencing fields near their settlements. In the decades before Hannah Freeman was born, her kin continued to move between their seasonal homes, taking advantage of the resources the lands and waters offered.[11] The Lenapes had an extensive and intimate knowledge of the weather, soils, and other critical variables relative to planting and harvesting crops, hunting, fishing, and gathering of local resources. In the spring Lenape families moved to their homes along the fertile river flatlands to clear fields and plant crops, which were harvested in the fall. Groups of women and girls gathered resources in the forests and wetlands within a day's walking distance from their farms. Hannah's father and uncles tended to their fishing and hunting camps according to the seasonal migrations of the game or fish they sought. One of the most important foods for the Brandywine Lenapes was shad, anadromous fish not unlike salmon that live in the ocean but swim upstream to spawn in the fresh waters of rivers and creeks. Every spring, from April to June, Lenape men used nets and weirs to catch the fish, which they dried and smoked for their families.[12] Despite the abundance that the Brandywine Lenapes enjoyed in the summer and fall, special care was always taken to prepare for the seasons when the land and river were more reluctant to give up their riches. In the fall after harvests, the fields were burned to fertilize the soil and make tracking animals easier. Burning the understory of the forest was a regular practice for the Lenapes because it thinned out invasive plants at the same time that it restored a healthy balance to the ecosystem that everyone depended on. Late in the year Lenape families would break into smaller groups and return to their winter homes as the days grew shorter and the temperatures dropped. Hunting parties of Lenape men left their homes to hunt deer, bear, waterfowl, and other animals for community consumption and trade. Beaver and deer pelts were in much demand by English traders, and the Brandywine men and women enjoyed the merchandise that the fur trade brought to their homes. During the winter months, women, children, and elders continued to work for their families and communities in a traditional seasonal round that had been practiced for generations.[13]

During the first decades of their cohabitation, the Lenapes and English living together in southeastern Pennsylvania enjoyed a relatively stable coexistence. Both peoples shared an interest in improving their access to economic opportunities and material goods made available through trade. Lenape women wore skirts made of cloth from England, and English women decorated their homes with woven mats and baskets made by Lenape women. Everyone cooked corn and made stews from local game and vegetables, but each preferred their own recipes and their own customs.[14] The Lenapes and English were both in the process of negotiating their place in a rapidly changing world. For the Lenapes, one of their origin stories is a story of migration. As a people they had traveled great distances in the

All Our Grandmothers

past, encountering adversity, loss, and enemies. Despite these obstacles they remained a collective people. Their story of migration is a story of movement, change, and diversity. Places and practices changed, but the people created new ideas and ways of living that in turn became Lenape ways. Their newest neighbors may have posed one of the greatest threats to their way of life, but the Lenapes endured. For their part, the English settlers were not unfamiliar with change. The Quaker immigrants who settled in the Brandywine River valley were in the process of creating their own story of migration as a people. They were following a spiritually driven path they hoped would result in a better world. They were less rigid than many of their colonial counterparts in recognizing their relationship to indigenous Americans through their belief that even the Lenapes possessed the "inner light." The spiritual purpose that led English, Welsh, and Irish Quakers to leave their own ancient homelands found footing in the leadership of a man who was committed to establishing a colony that promoted the fair and respectful treatment of the indigenous inhabitants.

In the months before his arrival in November 1682, William Penn put much thought into planning and promoting his vision of the new colony. A large part of that vision concerned the Lenape peoples and their place in Penn's new world. Soon after the charter was confirmed, Penn wrote a letter to the "inhabitants of Pennsylvania." His letter was not intended for the Lenapes, but for the other English, Dutch, and Swedish settlers who made their homes within Penn's boundaries. At that time the new colony had fewer than two thousand European settlers, but Penn wanted to assure them that he would protect "whatever sober and freemen can reasonably desire" in their new government.[15] He had not yet been to Pennsylvania, but in a series of promotional pamphlets he expressed ideas that were common among sixteenth- and seventeenth-century colonizers. He stated that colonies were the "seeds of nations" and would increase the wealth and prosperity of the king and his subjects. He cited historical precedent from Christian scriptures to texts of the ancient Greeks and Romans arguing that English settlers would spread civilization to their newly subject lands and "reduce" the native inhabitants by conquering their "barbarity."[16] From England Penn had arranged the first sales of land in Pennsylvania and also instructed the first purchasers that only he had the authority to purchase and clear titles to Indian lands in the colony. He also set out a series of rules regarding Indian trade. One of Penn's primary objectives in his instructions to the first purchasers was to prevent any disputes or subsequent hostilities with the Indians living in the boundaries of his new colony. Along with controlling land and trade sales, from his home in England he laid the groundwork for the legal status of Indians in his colony. Penn declared that any unprovoked wrong done to an Indian by a settler would be treated "as if he had committed it against his fellow planter" and that any such grievances must be taken to the local authority, magistrate, deputy, or the governor, who "shall to his utmost of his power take care with the king of the said Indian." Further, Penn magnanimously declared that the "Indians shall have liberty to do all things relating to the improvement of their ground" that his own settlers were permitted to do.[17] Clearly, the Indian peoples living in Pennsylvania were not English subjects, but Penn unmistakably placed them under his judicial and political authority. Although he did seek their consent in land sales by acquiring signatures on purchases, like other colonial authorities Penn took no steps to subject the indigenous Americans to the English Crown. In fact, Penn encouraged their separateness and sovereignty.

The Brandywine Lenapes never granted William Penn ownership of their lands because it was never theirs to give. The Lenapes, like most indigenous peoples in North America, did not conceive of land as a commodity to trade or sell. Lenapes understood the earth as a living entity—people were not separate from it but a part of it. Like Europeans they had boundaries and borders around areas that were used in common by fami-

All Our Grandmothers

3. Gustavus Hesselius, *Lapowinska*, 1735, a rare portrait of a Lenape sachem contemporary with Hannah Freeman. (Courtesy of the Philadelphia History Museum at the Atwater Kent, the Historical Society of Pennsylvania Collection)

lies, communities, and larger politically organized groups such as confederacies and councils, but Indian properties were not delineated in ways that Europeans recognized. Fields were not fenced in and gates and walls did not restrict the movements of

4. Gustavus Hesselius, *Tishcohan*, 1735, a rare portrait of an eighteenth-century Lenape leader. (Courtesy of the Philadelphia History Museum at the Atwater Kent, the Historical Society of Pennsylvania Collection)

peoples from one place to another. Instead they knew the borders of their lands by paths, tree lines, boulders, rivers, and other natural features. Some of these natural markers were imbued with sacred qualities and others were permanent features that

All Our Grandmothers

left little doubt regarding meaning to those who had long histories in that place. The Brandywine Lenapes, like many of their Algonquian neighbors in the eastern woodlands of North America, shared space with other Native peoples and were not unfamiliar with the disputes that could arise over fishing, hunting, and rights of settlement. Ceremonies, negotiations, and gifts mediated those disputes. And when those avenues failed they, not unlike Europeans, resorted to open hostilities. The Delaware River is a good example of a Lenape territorial boundary. The fall line in the Delaware River marks the geographic distinction between the uplands and the lower Piedmont by rocks and rapids in the river. For the Lenape this physical boundary was an ancient border between their related communities, evidenced by the distinction between different dialects of their language: Unami to the south of the fall line and Munsee to the north.[18]

Cultural understanding between Quakers and Lenapes was possible along many paths. Boundaries and territories were equally important to William Penn and the Lenapes, but both cultures expressed and managed those ideas differently. Land tenure and rights of occupations were valuable to both peoples, but those rights and claims were expressed differently in the first decades of contact. Lenape sachems in Pennsylvania and William Penn also found common cause in a shared peace ethic. The sachems and Penn valued peaceful coexistence and exchange over war, and representatives of both cultures worked diligently to that end. William Penn did not create a "peaceable kingdom" so much as he settled in one that predated his arrival. The Brandywine and other Lenapes living throughout the Delaware River valley understood the importance of peaceful solutions when confronted with challenges to their political and economic security. The Susquehannocks, an Iroquoian-speaking people, began to immigrate into Lenape territories during the mid-sixteenth century, not long before the first Dutch and Swedish settlers began building forts along Delaware Bay. They acted as a powerful conduit to the northern fur trade, and the colonists were eager to participate in that trade. Subsequently, the Lenapes found themselves pressed on their eastern and western boundaries by outsiders who threatened the stability and safety of the Lenape villages. Occasional violence did erupt, but for the most part the Lenape sachems negotiated successfully for a peaceful coexistence with their new Native and European neighbors. The foundation of their success was finding an economic and political niche that preserved their village-based autonomy and control over the lands and resources throughout the region.[19] Through trial and error and astute observations of their competitors and adversaries, they understood that their power rested in their ability to exploit the needs of both the Susquehannocks and the Europeans. Providing food, alliances and loyalty, and a variety of diplomatic and communications services as messengers and guides allowed the Lenapes to create a successful political, cultural, and economic niche in the region. Initially they found little reason to resist the offers of friendship and peace that William Penn's agent delivered in August 1681. From the Lenapes' perspective, he and his fellow Quakers were only the latest members of an interconnected network of trade and alliances.

In the late summer of 1681, over a year before Penn's own arrival, William Markham arrived with specific instructions for governing the colony and conducting business. Among his first acts was the delivery of a letter from Penn addressed to the "Kings of the Indians." The letter is brief and to the point. Penn begins by proclaiming that there was "one great God" who governed them all, Lenape and European alike. He goes on to explain that it was through his god's guidance that he was "concerned in your parts of the world" and that the "king of the country where I live has given unto me a great province," namely, the Lenape lands. Despite Penn's presumptions about the Lenapes' shared belief in "one great God," it is not difficult to imagine how the Lenape sachems understood the situation based on the actions of Penn's emissary. Markham came to the Lenapes in friend-

All Our Grandmothers

ship, participated in ceremonies, offered hospitality, and exchanged gifts. Penn's agent employed a well-known local Swedish trader, guide, and interpreter, Lasse Cock, to translate the absent proprietor's message. Markham presented the Lenapes with guns, powder, matchcoats, and stroudwater, a red and blue woolen cloth made in England that was popular among Native consumers.[20] From the Lenapes' point of view, the Englishmen clearly understood the regional protocol and diplomacy. There was nothing new in Markham's presentation to alarm local Indian leaders or to suggest a major deviation from their earlier trade and land dealings with Europeans.

But popular accounts of Pennsylvania's founding would have us believe otherwise. William Penn and his colonial enterprise are presented as "unique" and "exceptional" in large part because of his relations with the Lenapes. This pervasive interpretation is situated largely in an analysis of treaties and corresponding documentation rather than in a Lenape account of events. As historian James O'Neil Spady stated, "There is no evidence that the Lenapes praised the benevolence or justice of William Penn's policy" and, in fact, if given the chance they might offer a story of "bitterness, disappointment, and loss" regarding their relationship with Pennsylvania's benevolent proprietor.[21] There is no doubt that Penn's commitment to pacifism inspired his desire to acquire Indian lands "with their love and consent" by purchasing Indian titles rather than by conquest. In his first address to the Lenape he explained, "I am very sensible of the unkindness and injustice that has been too much exercised toward you" by his countrymen's willingness to "make great advantage" of the generosity of local Native communities.[22]

While part of Penn's ideology rested on his spiritual ideals, he was also well schooled in the successes and failures of other English colonies. In 1675 New England colonists fought a yearlong war against the Wampanoags under the leadership of their grand sachem, Metacom. King Philip's War, titled so for Metacom's English name, devastated the countryside, costing the colony in lives, property, and much-needed revenue. Ultimately, the colonists defeated Metacom and his followers, but only after months of retreat and evacuation of their newly settled towns and hamlets. Similarly, to the south, Chesapeake farmers, aggravated by disputes over property and land with local Indians, escalated to unprovoked violence against all Indians living in Virginia. When Governor Berkley ordered the settlers to stop the attacks, Nathaniel Bacon took the rebellion to the colonial capital at Jamestown, forcing the governor to evacuate the town. Eventually Bacon's Rebellion was suppressed and its perpetrators hanged, but the lesson was not lost on William Penn. From his perspective, warfare with Indians was not only morally wrong; it was costly. The most expedient way to prevent hostilities between English settlers and the Lenapes was to purchase lands, clear their titles according to English customs, and maintain tight control over the colony's expansion. William Penn was no fool. Within months of his first letter to the Indians, he sent further instructions to Markham, urging him to "treat speedily with the Indians for land before they are furnished by others with things that please them."[23] William Penn understood that he held no exceptional place in the hearts of local Lenape leadership and that there were others who competed for the Lenapes' "love and consent."

In April 1682 William Markham negotiated the first purchase of Lenape lands on behalf of William Penn in southeastern Pennsylvania. It took several months before the terms of the exchange were finalized, but on July 15, 1682, twelve sachems signed the formal deed for lands that included the future site of Philadelphia and Penn's personal estate further north up the Delaware River. The deed contained all of the redundancies and assurances expected in an English legal document. We can never be certain how the Lenapes understood the language and meaning of the parchment they signed or if they truly comprehended the implications of the agreement. From the English perspective, the Lenape sachems and "their heirs

All Our Grandmothers

and assigns" quitted any "right, title, interest, use, property, and claim" to their former lands "forevermore." With their signatures William Penn asserted sole ownership of all "islands, rivers, rivulets, creeks, waters, ponds, lakes, plains, hills, mountains, meadows, marshes, swamps, trees, woods, mines, minerals" contained in the lands described in the deed. There is much debate regarding whether the Lenapes understood these early purchases as agreements to share the use of the lands or as the complete loss of control, rights, and access, as the English purchasers understood it. But in a very short time, the Lenape communities would come to fully understand what the Englishmen meant by taking possession "forevermore."[24]

Between December 1681 and December 1682, twenty-three ships burdened with cargo and passengers made their landings along the Delaware River. Each ship carried approximately two thousand passengers: men, women, and children, some Quaker, many not. Most came from England, Ulster, or Protestant Germany, but among them were settlers from Wales, Scotland, France, and the Netherlands. The majority came from the upwardly mobile but middle part of the population. Most were skilled in trades or farming and often came as families. The wealthier merchants and landed aristocrats did not want to make what was often a dangerous voyage to North America, and the poor and destitute had no means to do so. Eventually the poor would make their way to Pennsylvania as indentured servants, and many would find the colony "the best poor man's country." William Penn's year of advertising and promoting the colony paid off, perhaps beyond his own expectations. Within a decade the population exploded, increasing from fewer than two thousand settlers to nine thousand in southeastern Pennsylvania, and by 1700 the number had more than doubled to twenty-one thousand inhabitants.[25]

Their previous experience living and trading with the earlier Dutch, Swedish, and English settlements did not prepare the Lenape sachems for the rapid changes Penn's colonial program brought to their homelands. Until the 1680s the Lenapes had successfully exploited their closeness to the small, scattered colonial settlements by increasing their own productivity of goods the settler market demanded. The fishing and hunting resources necessary to sustain their own communities were largely untouched. Their freedom to travel across the countryside was unhindered by their European neighbors, and they enjoyed the access to trade goods made available by the settlements. This is not to suggest that life in late seventeenth-century southeastern Pennsylvania was idyllic. Violence, disease, hunger, and conflict were part of colonial life, for Indians and foreigners alike. But the rapidity with which Penn and his agents parceled and sold lands and the unrivaled pace at which the lots were occupied by the newcomers not only challenged Penn's plans to maintain tight control of his colony, it forced new realities upon the Lenape communities that agreed to sign the treaties offered by Penn and his agents.

By 1682 William Markham had made remarkable progress fulfilling the proprietor's instructions. In successive purchases Markham acquired Lenape lands contiguous to each earlier purchase, extending the colonial lands north and south along the western bank of the Delaware River. After his arrival Penn took the lead in negotiating with Lenape sachems and was an active participant in most of the land purchases. He made earnest attempts to learn the Lenape language but still relied on a corps of Lenape, Swedish, and English translators in the recorded meetings. In the summer of 1683 he acquired three more tracts of land from sachems representing Lenape communities within the boundaries of the Neshaminy Creek to the north and Chester Creek to the south. Penn, acting as the sole agent, held complete authority to negotiate the boundaries and purchases with the consent of the king and with the help of his surveyors, interpreters, and various witnesses. Lenape sachems acquired the power and authority to negotiate the sale of their lands and the acceptance of payment from a very different source. As Wil-

All Our Grandmothers

liam Penn observed, "It is admirable to consider how powerful the kings [Lenape sachems] are, and yet how they move by the breath of their people."[26]

The Lenapes did not have a king with absolute authority; they were politically organized around smaller, separate autonomous communities. The leaders of their communities in the late seventeenth century were called sachems. Sachems did not rule as kings, even though Penn and other English negotiators would insist on recognizing them as such. It was difficult for English colonials to acknowledge or understand the ways in which Lenapes and other indigenous Americans organized themselves politically. Sachems expressed authority, but their power did not rest in the subordination of other members of their society beneath them. The power and authority of Lenape sachems rested in their wisdom, generosity, and the collective knowledge of the community. In many meetings between Lenape leaders and colonial officials throughout this period, the sachems and their messengers repeatedly demonstrated their philosophy for the English in attendance. "We rule from our heart and not from our head" was the declaration performed by the speaker, who would strike his own head and heart multiple times to demonstrate his meaning for all in attendance. Colonial observers rarely understood the depth of the sachems' proclamation, seeing only a ritual performance to be endured.

During this period Lenape sachems rose to their position of authority either by maternal lineage or because they had proven to be someone of extraordinary wisdom suited to serve as a leader. Unlike Penn and those who stood to profit from the acquisition of land, Lenape sachems sought trade goods and payments for their lands in order to distribute the wealth to their communities. Penn, an eyewitness and careful observer of Lenape sachems, noted that "wealth circulates like blood, all parts partake." Further, he commented on the Lenapes' generosity: "Nothing is too good for their friend. Give them a fine gun, coat or other thing, it may pass twenty hands before it sticks."[27] The

Lenapes' political world also included a head or grand sachem who spoke for the people in negotiations with colonists, but he acted only on the consent of his council, which was comprised of the "old and wise" of his community.

When the sachems met to discuss terms of the land purchases or trade agreements the occasion was a public event in which many members of the Lenape communities were involved. The meetings often took place in Philadelphia, sometimes at the Quaker Meeting House and other times at a convenient location such as a trader's house. Penn and his counselors, as was their custom, sat in chairs behind tables, parchments, pens, and inkwells spread about to record the event. The English presented their terms, publicly proclaimed in English followed by a translation for the Lenape members of the audience. The Lenape head sachem sat on the ground in the center of his people, surrounded in concentric half circles by his advisors, the young warriors, the elders, both men and women, and their families. After deliberations, the sachem's spokesperson delivered his response to the English. During one such negotiation, Penn noted that when the sachem's message was spoken, the room was silent, "not a man among them was observed to whisper or smile; the old, the grave, the young, reverent in their deportment." In this particular exchange, Penn offered all his customary overtures of "peace and good neighborhood'" but privately, sounding just a bit envious, he complained that the Lenapes had raised the price of land from previous negotiations. "I have never seen more natural sagacity . . . and he will disserve the name of wise that outwits them in any treaty."[28]

On November 19, 1683, William Penn negotiated and signed an agreement for lands lying between Chester Creek and Christina River, including the Brandywine River. Among those who met with Penn and entered into the preliminary negotiations was Secetareus, the principal sachem of the Brandywine Lenapes. During this meeting the Brandywine sachem and five others initiated an agreement promising to sell the lands "in ye

All Our Grandmothers

5. George Lehman, *The Great Elm Tree of Shackamaxon*, 1830. (Courtesy of the American Philosophical Society, Philadelphia)

Spring next." In the agreement Secetareus also acknowledged that he was in possession of partial payment for the land, including a "very good gun, some powder and lead, two pairs of stockings, one matchcoat and ten bits of Spanish money."[29] In 1685 a deed was issued confirming the exchange that included a more complete inventory of the terms of payment but also acknowledged a complaint regarding the agreement. Apparently settlers were building dams on the lower sections of their river that prevented the shad from making their seasonal runs upstream. The shad were of vital importance to Hannah's ancestors and a central part of their diet in season. In many complaints to Penn's agents in Philadelphia, Secetareus and his successor, Checochinican, argued that the colonial settlers were in violation of the terms of their agreement: the Brandywine River was supposed to remain open and unencumbered. By 1690 settlers on the lower reaches of the river had built several dams for sawing lumber and mills for grinding grain. Penn was right when he said the Lenapes were sagacious. They registered their complaint with the Board of Property in Philadelphia, which in turn sent a letter ordering the settlers to remove their dams.[30]

William Penn returned to England in 1684 after only two short years in his much-loved colony. It would be another fifteen years before he returned. All together Penn lived in his colony only four years, but his legacy, both myth and fact, is built largely on his relationship with the Lenapes. There are two tales of William Penn that bear directly on the lives of Hannah Freeman and the Lenapes along the Brandywine River. One looms large in the traditional accounts of colonial Pennsylvania, well known by Pennsylvanian schoolchildren. The other is a story supported by evidence but not considered significant to the history of William Penn and his colony.

According to legend William Penn held a meeting at Shackamaxon sometime in the fall of 1682. Shackamaxon was formerly a Lenape town just north of Philadelphia's center and the site of much interaction between the local Lenapes and colonial settlers because of its advantageous position on the west bank of the Delaware River. The home of Swedish trader and interpreter Lasse Cock, the town was a familiar setting to the colonists and Lenapes, who could not have imagined the place Shackamaxon would take in modern historical imagination. The tradition tells us that Penn met with the Lenapes under a large elm tree to sign a treaty of peace. Benjamin West's 1771–72 painting *Penn's Treaty with the Indians* immortalized the mythical meeting. The artist's rendering interpreted Penn's benevolent colonialism as "a conquest that was made over native people without sword or dagger."[31] An early account reported that Penn appeared under the spreading branches of an "elm tree of prodigious size" dressed in the simple plain clothes of a Quaker, distinguished by a "sky-blue sash" worn about his waist. Surrounding Penn beneath the treaty elm sat the "lawless sav-

6. Benjamin West, *Penn's Treaty with the Indians*, 1771–72. (Courtesy of the Pennsylvania Academy of the Fine Arts, Philadelphia. Gift of Mrs. Sarah Harrison [the Joseph Harrison Jr. Collection])

ages . . . attending in great numbers . . . as far as the eye could discern painted and armed." Penn, unarmed, stood center stage with arms open, a parchment in one hand. As the story goes, he made a brief speech offering peace and friendship and followed his words with gifts and trade. He presented a parchment to the head sachem and asked that it be preserved "for three generations, that their children might know what had passed." According to this early historian, "This treaty forms a brilliant ray of the halo which graces the head of William Penn."[32] Artists, poets, philosophers, and academics absorbed and amplified this story despite there being no eyewitness accounts or indeed any documentary proof that it ever happened. Nonetheless, the legend continues to be widely accepted and celebrated to this day.

What we do know is that during the two short years Penn spent in Pennsylvania during his first trip he was an extremely active administrator and conducted numerous meetings with Lenapes throughout the region. More than one meeting took place at Shackamaxon, but in the historical imagination the numerous meetings, negotiations, challenges, and complaints are condensed into one single meeting that elevated William Penn to a near-saint status. Emphasis on his pacifist policies overshadowed the fact that he was introducing an aggressive program of land acquisition that dispossessed the majority of Lenapes of their historic homelands in southeastern Pennsylvania.[33]

The bucolic image celebrated in the West painting and the subsequent civic canonization of Penn silence the history of the Lenapes and other Indians who made Pennsylvania their home. The meaning and significance of the treaties negotiated between William Penn, his agents, and the sachems representing the Lenape communities are obscured beneath the "brilliant halo" of an embedded mythology. While Penn is not responsible for his subsequent canonization in Pennsylvania's origin story, he nevertheless sought to "reduce" the Lenapes on their land and expressed his vision for the Lenapes in assimilationist terms. Penn believed in the intrinsic superiority of English culture and promoted the expansion of English power. The language of brotherhood and friendship often expressed by Penn was genuine to a point, but he operated from an assumption that he was introducing an improved mode of living and hoped that his disciplined and well-ordered colonists would serve as living examples to emulate. Penn appreciated the innate spirituality of the Lenape peoples and admired many qualities about them, an opinion that few of his fellow English settlers shared. Nevertheless, Penn's limited admiration proceeded from a cultural worldview that assumed the Lenapes were an inferior culture. Despite the common ground Lenapes and Quakers shared, this belief was paramount over all others. The spirit of cooperation and stability between the Lenapes and the Quakers did not last long. As thousands and thousands of settlers fenced, farmed, and restricted access to the resources of the Lenapes' homelands, the discord between the Native community and Penn's benevolent colonialism increased.

All Our Grandmothers

The other story, unlike the mythologized account of the treaty at Shackamaxon under the spreading elm tree, is rooted in documentary evidence. But it is a story that rarely, if ever, receives the attention accorded to accounts that sanctify William Penn's colonial Indian policies. The story concerns the resistance to English expansion of Checochinican, head sachem of Hannah Freeman's people. When Checochinican stepped into a role of leadership formerly held by Secetareus, he had most likely witnessed or in some peripheral way participated in the negotiations that included the Brandywine Lenapes' lands. It is easy to assume that Secetareus and William Penn knew each other. Penn personally negotiated purchases concerning the lands along the Brandywine. He also mentions Secetareus in his letter to the Free Society of Traders in 1683, and later, upon his return to England, he sent back a cap as a gift to the Lenape leader. In the elder sachem's savvy negotiations with Penn, boundaries were specified to reserve land for one mile on either side of the Brandywine River, from the mouth where it empties into Delaware Bay north to the branch in the river and then continuing up the west branch to the falls. Penn guaranteed that Hannah's people would "not be molested . . . from generation to generation."[34] Secetareus, understanding how vital the river and its fertile bottomlands were to his people, did not sell those lands to William Penn or his agents.

At around the same time Penn acknowledged another grant of land that can only be understood as a reservation. The Okehocking Lenapes agreed to settle on a specific parcel of land that was eventually bordered and surrounded on all sides by settlers' tracts. In 1701 the commissioners of property issued a deed for 500 acres within a larger tract of 1,920 acres that were originally surveyed for one of the early Quaker purchasers, Griffith Jones. For an unknown reason, Jones never settled on the property and so it reverted back to public lands controlled by William Penn. Remember that Penn was exercising absolute authority over the sale of lands as much as he could and in this particular circumstance, as he did with Secetareus, he set aside a portion of these lands for the Lenapes' use. Quaker Nathaniel Newlin participated in both the Brandywine and Jones surveys, and in the latter case he was charged with designating an allotment suitable "for settlement for the [Okehocking] Indians."[35]

The Okehocking Lenapes consolidated their communities in the face of rapid settlement, similar to Hannah's Brandywine community. The lands Penn set aside were lands they historically occupied as their summer locations. It is important to remember that the Lenapes moved between various permanent locations: winter hunting camps, spring and summer planting fields, fish camps, ceremonial grounds, and other dispersed locations. Anytime Lenapes vacated one of their settlements, even if only for a month or two, land-hungry settlers seized the opportunity to purchase lands they claimed had been abandoned by the Indians. From their perspective it was ethical and legal. Penn's stipulation was that any "unoccupied" lands reverted to public properties that could then be sold to interested buyers. There were no time limits on the abandonment, even though most local settlers were clearly aware of the Lenapes' seasonal occupations. The Okehocking Lenapes, who had previously lived in various locations along several tributary streams, lost access to many of their settlements and camps in increments as settlers moved onto lands they deemed abandoned and available for purchase. The Okehocking sachems agreed to the terms of the reservation boundaries because it was the only viable option for protecting and preserving a portion of their former lands from further dispossession. Day to day, individuals and communities made decisions to protect and preserve their homelands, always with an eye toward avoiding conflict and providing for their people.

The Brandywine and Okehocking settlements are unique in the early colonization of Pennsylvania. In all other cases, land-purchase agreements between the colonial government and the Indian leadership usually designated the borders of the property that contained, encompassed, and limited the *colonial settlement.* In the case of the Okehocking and Brandywine deeds, both presented terms that put specific boundaries all around *Indian lands,* making them an encircled minority within the ever-increasing settler populations. By 1700 it was clear that the balance of power in southeastern Pennsylvania had shifted to favor colonial expansion. The Lenapes responded in a variety of ways. Many chose this time to relocate further west and north toward the Susquehanna River in order to put distance between them and Pennsylvania's settlers. Others continued to live on lands protected by earlier agreements, choosing to deal with the problems associated with living so near to colonial settlements, including violence, the alcohol trade, and the limitations on their former way of life.

As the Okehocking Lenapes adjusted to the limitations of living in a fixed and narrowly confined reservation, the Brandywine Lenapes faced similar threats to their own protected lands. Between 1683 and 1692 Secatareus and other sachems settled on terms that gave the commissioners of property access to survey and parcel lands that extended from Chester Creek on the eastern border to Christiana Creek on the western side. Within this boundary Penn set aside a reserve for Secatareus and the Brandywine Lenapes, but within a very short time after Penn left the colony for England in 1684, the commissioners of property ordered surveys taken of those same lands. There is no evidence to explain why they took actions that directly impinged Penn's agreement regarding the Brandywine reserve. One possible explanation is that the commissioners of property acted in good faith, not being aware that Penn had made an exception or separate agreement regarding the property in question. On the other hand, they may have known about the exception but, as with the Okehocking Lenapes, had deemed seasonal absence from the land a signal of their right to parcel the abandoned settlements. What is evident is that beginning in 1685 the commissioners of property sold parcels on both the east and west side of the Brandywine River. Among the first purchasers are the very families that became intimately involved in Hannah Freeman's life: Harlan, Barnard, Chandler, Pierce, Webb, and Marshall.

Checochinican did not sit quietly by as Quaker settlers took possession of the Lenapes' protected lands. In 1701 George Harlan petitioned the commissioners of property to purchase a parcel within the Lenapes' reserve. Harlan was already living on lands adjacent to the reserve in 1690 and probably knew his neighbors and their habits fairly well. According to the petition, Harlan claimed that he, "having been long helpful to the Indians in fencing and improving a settlement made by them for some years back . . . requests a grant of 200 acres of that land over against his plantation where the said Indians were settled, but have now left it."[36] Since the Lenapes were not fencing their own fields at this time, we can only assume that the fencing and improving he claimed to have done for the Indians was in fact completed to separate his property from theirs. It is also not unreasonable to suspect that Harlan may have been taking advantage of the Lenapes' seasonal absences to occupy and claim lands not legally open to settler occupation. The petition does not clarify how long the property was vacant, nor is it known if there was any attempt made to contact Checochinican to confirm Harlan's report. Even more significant is that Harlan's petition for the land was granted in just over a week; he received the warrant to survey and purchase the land. When the Lenapes returned to this rich bottomland in the spring, according to Hannah's account, they "were no longer able to plant corn."[37]

We do not know Checochinican's immediate response, but by 1705 the Brandywine Lenapes were registering their official objections to the commissioners by restating the claim that they were granted sole rights to all of the lands, one mile on each bank from the north branch of the Brandywine to the mouth of the river. In 1706 the commissioners of property could not ignore the illegality of the warrants issued to Harlan and oth-

All Our Grandmothers

er settlers and acknowledged "the repeated complaints of the inhabitants of Brandywine whose lands have never been purchased of the Indians" and "agreed with Checochinican the chief of the said Indians there to buy off their claims for one hundred pounds of Penn's money."[38] Checochinican had little choice but to accept this settlement. Between 1701, when the Brandywine Lenapes filed their official complaint, and 1706, when the commissioners offered the monetary compensation to Checochinican, Quaker settlers had fenced, built homes and barns, and taken possession of lands that legally still belonged to the Brandywine Lenapes. Once settlers took possession of the lands, legally or not, there was nothing short of warfare or forced removal that would dislodge the squatters. Checochinican negotiated the best settlement possible and sold those lands already illegally occupied by settlers. This parcel extended from the Brandywine's mouth where it met the Christiana River at the colony's southern boundary to the northern boundary, marked by a well-known rock adjacent to Abraham Marshall's land. Important to subsequent actions, Moses Marshall, one of Hannah Freeman's benefactors, inherited part of this parcel from his grandfather Abraham.

The colonial commissioners' failure to uphold Penn's original agreement with the Brandywine Lenapes was no minor affair. Eventually, in 1706, James Logan, one of the commissioners, informed William Penn "about a very troublesome claim of the Indians to land on the Brandywine, reserved at their great sale." Checochinican was a savvy sachem. He negotiated what he and the members of his council believed was the best option for their communities, an agreement very similar to the actions taken by the Okehocking community. He sold the lands already lost to illegal occupation, seeking the best compensation possible. Monetarily, the negotiations were less than satisfying from the sachem's perspective. He received a promise of 100 pounds, which was "a third only of what they insisted on."[39] But although he did not get the price he wanted, he did score a political coup of sorts. He forced the colonial authorities to admit the illegality of their actions and also to reconfirm and document the boundaries of the lands remaining under the Brandywine Lenapes' control. This would be critical to the future of Hannah Freeman and her family.

The agreement between Checochinican and the commissioners of property made in 1706 did not settle the issue for long. In the following decade Checochinican and other Brandywine Lenapes continued to register complaints, largely about the building of dams on the lower part of the river. In 1721 Checochinican and his wife made an especially memorable appearance during a diplomatic visit to Governor Keith. Checochinican by this time was a well-known Lenape leader and "had won both respect and love among the English." Checochinican entered the hall followed in single file by a group of his best warriors. The sachem was simply attired, as were his men, and the English were in awe of his demeanor and appearance. According to one eyewitness, "King Checochinican went in front bare headed, as they all go, having only in their lock of hair a large silk red ribbon which hung over their back." He wore a blue and white "four cornered cloth quilt" and "red-winged moccasins on his feet." After the sachem's retinue filed past the governor, his wife presented herself, followed by a procession of the important women of the community. Like her husband, she exhibited an air of authority and character admired by the English witnesses, who noted that she too was dressed simply, like the other Lenape women, except that she wore a "black quilt which she carried over one shoulder."[40] Not long after this diplomatic meeting, Checochinican initiated a formal complaint that colonial officials were unable to ignore.

In 1725 Checochinican requested a formal audience in order to make a complaint to the provincial assembly regarding intrusions on the lands belonging to the Brandywine Lenapes. During this formal hearing the sachem reminded the gathered assemblymen of Penn's promise of "perpetual friendship" and

All Our Grandmothers

that "after we sold him our country he re-conveyed back a certain tract of land upon the Brandywine for one mile on each side of said creek." Checochinican explained that they did not have the document because it was lost in a cabin fire, but "we all remember well the contents thereof." Checochinican went on to give an oral account of the document's contents, adding that "now it is not half the age of an old man since, and we are molested, and our lands surveyed out and settled before we can reap our corn off; and to our great injury."[41] He stated his case against the settlers clearly and succinctly. It is easy to imagine the sachem of the Brandywine Lenapes, a beloved leader of his people and equally well respected among the Quakers, standing before the assembly making accusations that struck at the core of William Penn's promise and also of Quaker ethics. In a rare moment, Checochinican brought to public attention a practice that the English settlers in Pennsylvania had embraced for a generation: illegal squatting as a means to legal possession. In particular the sachem complained that the river was "so obstructed with dams, that the fish cannot come up to our habitations . . . we desire that these dams be removed, that the fish can have their natural course." The speaker of the assembly asked Checochinican if he expected to "enjoy that land forever." Checochinican must have been surprised at such a question but quickly responded, "Not only we, but all the Indians understood it to be theirs as long as the water ran down the creek." He ended his address by firmly stating that if steps were not taken to rectify the situation, he would "be obliged to come again next Spring."[42]

The assembly members discussed the situation privately and determined a formal course of action to handle the complaint. Initially they reported the sachem's testimony to James Logan, one of the commissioners of property. After some consideration he agreed that Checochinican had a valid claim against Harlan and the other settlers. Logan also suggested that the settlers who had illegally purchased the Lenapes lands be persuaded to release their claims in exchange for other available properties. Logan, formerly William Penn's personal secretary, clearly understood the gravity and validity of the sachem's complaint. Logan was a shrewd businessman who held multiple positions within Penn's colony from the beginning and was the "defacto superintendent of Indian affairs" for the colony.[43] It is unlikely he would have so quickly offered compensation if he had not believed the truth of the petition. Logan also offered his own account of the events, explaining that the sachem and his council had repeatedly made this complaint, but nothing had yet been done to stop the settlers' encroachment. Once again William Penn's promise was central to the issue, and the sachem and his counselors reminded Logan that they "never sold their land . . . never sold the water." Even more important, the sachem detailed the impact of the settlers' actions on his communities, telling Logan that "if they are thrown out of this small possession . . . their children must be vagabonds without any home or living." Checochinican was only demanding what his people were promised: the right to be protected on their own lands, the right to live peaceably among the settlers and to remain friends with their colonial neighbors in Penn's "peaceable kingdom." Checochinican and the Brandywine Lenapes never broke that promise, but those who inherited William Penn's colony did.

Checochinican explicitly pointed out the illegal actions of one particular Quaker, Nathaniel Newlin. In modern terms Newlin was a real estate developer. He was a skilled surveyor working for the government and also an investor, purchasing large lots as they became available. He then subdivided the property and made his profit selling lots to the endless stream of settlers disembarking in Philadelphia. Newlin understood the promises made to the Lenapes. If you will recall, he was one of the surveyors who determined the boundaries of the lands most suitable for the Okehocking band to settle on in 1701. Checochinican accused Newlin of being "unkind" because he was dis-

All Our Grandmothers

covered covertly marking property lines with small nicks in the trees. According to the sachem, diplomatic protocol demanded that Newlin should have come to the sachem's town to "acquaint them" with what he was doing. Logan responded that "the commissioners were sorry to hear any complaint made of Nathaniel Newlin who had been an old settler in the country and a good friend of William Penn."[44] The commissioners, acting upon Logan's response, prepared a report for Governor Keith endorsing the validity of the Lenapes' complaint. They asked the governor to use his authority to resolve the situation before it led to open hostilities, which everyone sought to avoid. The commissioners hoped they could persuade Newlin to vacate the lands he illegally occupied and "becomes sensible" that it was in his own best interest to give up his illegal occupation of Lenape lands. Further, Governor Keith stated that he was traveling to the southern counties and would order the dismantling of any dams on the lower rivers that interfered with the Lenapes' access to fishing.

In the spring of 1726, Checochinican returned to the assembly and reported that Newlin had not removed himself from the Lenape lands and that the rivers remained encumbered by dams downstream. The Lenapes returned a report submitted to them by James Logan and stated they were not satisfied. After Checochinican's appearance in Philadelphia, the assembly scrambled to find out what exactly had been done to resolve the issue. Since the sachem's last visit the previous year, three witnesses had been identified who gave testimonies that supported the Lenapes' claim. Thomas Chandler, Alphonsus Kirk, and Samuel Hollingsworth were three of the Brandywine River's oldest Quaker residents and all lived on lands adjacent to the river that were part of the original Lenape tract. Not only did they acknowledge that Checochinican's complaint against Newlin was legitimate, but all three had personally seen the now-missing treaty signed and sealed by Penn and Markham. Nathaniel Newlin was also called to give a deposition. He declared he had no intention of causing harm to Checochinican and his people and was "heartily sorry" they were dissatisfied with his actions. More important, Newlin promised that "he will not give them any manner or disturbance in their uneasiness in their possessions . . . and will fully make good to them without any infraction."[45] The commissioner supported his deposition, saying that *if* Newlin lost his claim the government would compensate him for his loss. Despite the witnesses, testimonies, and Newlin's admission, the assembly seemed to be in doubt of the Lenapes' claim, which might explain why no further action occurred on the matter until Checochinican appeared in Philadelphia the following spring.

The day after Checochinican's appearance at the assembly to resubmit his complaint, James Logan gave a report in his capacity as commissioner of property that summed up the official findings. Logan claimed that while he was unable to find the specific deed remembered by the witnesses, both Quaker and Lenape testimonies were convincing. Logan acknowledged that the Brandywine Lenapes had legal right to all the land, one mile on each side, from the rock adjacent to Marshall's property to the head of the western branch. He also clarified that the lands from the same rock south to the mouth of the river were sold in 1705 "for the sum of one hundred, seventy-three pounds and eight shillings . . . which was . . . paid yesterday." Not only did Logan and the assembly acknowledge the legality of Checochinican's claim and that the payment for the other part of the parcel was twenty-five years late, they sent the sergeant at arms to bring Newlin to the hearing. Newlin signed a sworn statement promising that "neither he nor his heirs will by any means, disturb or molest" the Brandywine Lenape living along the river. Checochinican was once again satisfied, but he wanted something else. He asked Logan and the commissioners to give him a signed and sworn copy of the tract as agreed on in 1705 so that in the future they would be "secure" in their land claim. Logan's response suggests a palpable lack of sincerity on his part. He passed the buck. He told Checochinican that

All Our Grandmothers

it was not in his power to prepare such a document. It *was* in his power as commissioner of property to produce just such a document, and his refusal suggests he understood exactly how Checochinican was being played. Both Logan and Newlin had reassured and guaranteed that the Brandywine Lenapes would not be "disturbed or molested," but neither resolved to vacate the lands occupied by the Quaker squatters.[46]

As late as 1730, Checochinican and other Lenapes sporadically returned to the assembly to revisit their claim and renew their complaint, but as the years passed forces were at work that muffled and diminished the Lenapes' voices. After William Penn's death in 1718, his heirs and agents continued to evoke the rhetoric of the "peaceable kingdom" while endorsing irregular land practices and encouraging illegal settlement on Indian lands. Wave after wave of new immigrants followed the fertile waterways deeper and deeper into lands formerly occupied by the Lenapes. Colonial land speculators and government agents sought the most expedient means to satisfy these demands. Complaints like Checochinican's on behalf of the Brandywine Lenapes were heard from other sachems who still lived on lands guaranteed by William Penn. As settlers' surrounded the major areas of Lenape settlement, the Indians' ability to live on those remaining lands became more and more tenuous. Many families and communities chose to leave the region, moving further north and west, away from immigrant settlements. In former times the Lenapes had welcomed colonial neighbors, but now those same settlers brought alcohol, violence, and depravation. By the 1730s the Brandywine Lenape community was one of three major settlements resisting the illegal encroachment on their lands. Likewise, the sachems leading major Lenape communities in the Tulpehocken valley along the upper Schuylkill River and the Lenapes living between the forks of the Lehigh and Delaware rivers appeared in Philadelphia, registered complaints, and did everything they could to demand that William Penn's promise continue to be honored.[47] Despite the persistence of the Lenape sachems and the courage of their peoples in ongoing efforts to protect their rights to live in their ancient homelands, political, economic, and demographic forces conspired against them.

Checochinican and the Brandywine Lenapes never forgot the betrayal of William Penn's promise. As late as 1751, the sachem's son, Nemacolin, who lived far to the west near present-day Pittsburgh, renewed the claim of the Brandywine Lenapes. Christopher Gist, an agent for the Ohio Company, sought shelter in Nemacolin's home while surveying the western lands. Nemacolin remarked that in the previous year Gist had brought him a message from the "great men in Virginia to inform us of a present from the great king over the water." Nemacolin asked Gist, "If you can bring news from the king to us, why can't you tell him something for me?" Nemacolin then proceeded to make the same complaint that his father had a generation earlier. Checochinican never sold the land, colonial settlers continued to illegally occupy the land, and until the lands were returned to the Brandywine "the people who lived on it could get no title to it." Gist ignored the complaint, but in 1763 Nemacolin once again made an attempt to reclaim the lands. According to James Kenny, a trader in western Pennsylvania, Nemacolin came to see him. Kenny was very familiar with the Brandywine claim. He had grown up along the Brandywine River, the son of Quaker parents. He remembered Checochinican and knew the validity of Nemacolin's claim, so he agreed to take the old Lenape east to Philadelphia to make his complaint. Unfortunately, Nemacolin became ill and never made it to Philadelphia. We can only imagine how the colonial assembly would have treated Checochinican's heir.[48]

When Hannah Freeman was a small child she had probably watched, along with her parents and grandparents, the departure of the Brandywine Lenapes from their beloved ancestral homeland. By 1730 Checochinican had led a majority of his people north and west to a settlement along the Susquehanna

All Our Grandmothers

River, in hopes they would be safe and prosperous once again. It was the beginning of a Lenape diaspora that would last for over a century, but it was another episode in an ancient story of change and adaptation. Checochinican left the river valley knowing that his people had not completely abandoned it, and he most likely found some peace in the knowledge that there would always be Lenapes living along the Brandywine River. Lenape families like Hannah's stayed on their homelands as placeholders for their people. They would be there to do the ceremonies. They would be there to care for the land as best they could. And they would be there as Lenapes when and if their kin returned home.

Both the Lenapes who moved west and those who stayed in Pennsylvania faced enormous changes that impacted every aspect of their society. Change was a dynamic part of their history as a people, and in the eighteenth century that characteristic, perhaps more than any other, was key to their persistence as a people, no matter where they called home. Hannah Freeman grew up as a Lenape woman along the Brandywine River valley and lived there all her life. Her childhood, adolescence, and adulthood were unlike anything her peoples could have anticipated. Her Lenape kin shaped her identity, ethics, and worldview, but her Quaker neighbors brought changes that she equally embraced and resisted. She may have often looked to the west and wondered about her people and how they fared far from their beloved river. In contrast, other Lenapes who followed roads that carried them to western Pennsylvania, Ohio, and the lands further west and north looked to the east and never forgot where they came from. Perhaps, like Nemacolin, they dreamed of a time when they could go home again. What is certain is that no matter where Checochinican's people lived, they never forgot that the Brandywine River valley was their home.

CHAPTER THREE

The Peaceable Kingdom

Every morning Hannah Marshall, a young Quaker girl, began her daily chores by grabbing the large wooden bucket that sat inside the front door of her family home.[1] From the time she was old enough to lift and carry the weight of the filled pail, it was her responsibility to go out to the front well and bring water that her mother would heat for cooking their breakfast and washing their plates. Early morning was an especially busy time for all the farming families who lived up and down the Brandy-wine River valley, and each season brought change to the daily routine, which began with the hustle and bustle that centered on the large, open hearth that was the heart of their sturdy family home. The stone hearth was cluttered with hanging hooks for cooking pots, tongs to retrieve the fry pans from the glowing embers, and the bellows necessary to keep the fire burning. By the time Hannah Marshall returned with fresh water, her mother had the embers stoked and the fire hot in order to prepare the family's first meal of the day, which usually included a bowl of cooked oats and bread slathered with her mother's sweet home-churned butter. Each day brought its routines and each member of the family played a part in the success of their farm and household. From sunrise to sunset and beyond, every family member in the Marshall household, including Hannah's younger brother Moses, contributed to the health and well-being of their family. In turn, their household achievements supported the economic stability of the rapidly expanding community of English Quakers to which they belonged. The Marshall family

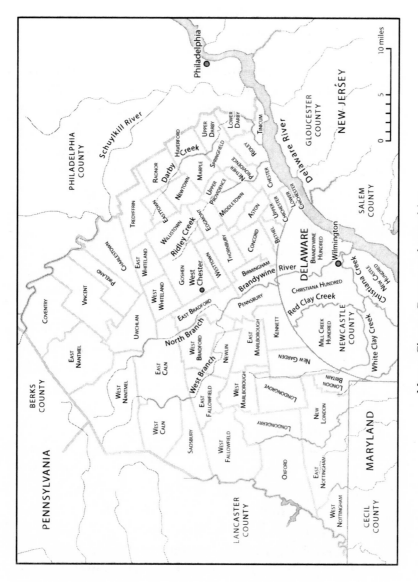

Map 2. Chester County and townships.

and many of their neighbors made their homes on some of the richest farmland in the thirteen colonies. But unlike many colonial settlers elsewhere, the residents of William Penn's colony enjoyed economic and political stability in the early decades of the eighteenth century. Hannah Marshall and her family experienced little deprivation in her lifetime, and the girl must have perceived a happy future from where she stood that early morning. She would come to learn her place and her responsibilities as a very young girl at her mother's side and make her own contributions to the security and stability of her Quaker community. As she stood gazing out at the Brandywine River that early morning, Hannah Marshall looked out upon a future full of promise. Did she or members of her family think about Hannah Freeman and the Lenape families who continued to make their living from the lands they shared? Hannah Marshall, like her brother Moses, knew Hannah Freeman all of her life and never forgot her Lenape neighbor. They were girls who walked the same wooded paths, probably worked together on local farms as the seasons demanded, and moved in and out of each other's lives, like so many other people living in this rural colonial community. Little did Hannah Marshall realize as she began her day's work that not far from that place of security, stability, and routine, her neighbor and friend faced a very different future.

Hannah Freeman lived a few short miles up the river from the Marshall homestead and looked out on the same physical landscape, but the young Lenape girl perceived this very differently from her neighbor. Her own history, the history of her people, was written on the hills, streams, and forests of the Brandywine River valley in unseen ways that the new settlers were unable to comprehend. She looked to the mountains in the distant northwest and knew that in a time before time, her people had made a generations-long journey to find their homeland in southeastern Pennsylvania.[2] She looked across the river and saw the burial ground where her ancestors lay, a sacred space she would someday share with all her grandmothers. Her history was intimately entwined with the river valley in a way that only she and her kin understood. But she also had much in common with her Quaker neighbor. Like Hannah Marshall, Hannah Freeman had daily chores and responsibilities that she learned beginning in her earliest years. Water was needed from the river, food had to be prepared, clothes needed mending—the work of daily subsistence awaited everyone in Chester County. But unlike that of her Quaker neighbors, Hannah's life was not so stable and her future was uncertain.

Hannah Freeman was born in a cabin on the property claimed by William Webb in the early spring of the year. Her exact birthday is not known, perhaps as early as 1720 or as late as 1730. Her family's cabin was situated along a small tributary of the Brandywine River known by the Quakers as Bennett's Run.[3] This fertile stretch of land, protected by dense forests, was the location of several reliable springs, an ideal location for her family's home. Local residents remembered the area as the "big woods" because of its isolation and pristine landscape.[4] William Webb claimed the land as his own, following the same pattern as many of his local neighbors. As was the case with the Harlan family, to which he was related by marriage, his title to the land originated in William Penn's first purchases from the Lenape Indians. Even though James Logan and the Pennsylvania Assembly had upheld Checochinican's challenge to the illegal parceling of the Brandywine lands in the 1720s, nothing was done to stem the tide of squatters who purchased tentative titles to the Lenapes' land. William Webb, like his neighbors, understood the history behind his land titles and showed little concern or interest in forcing Hannah Freeman's family from their small homestead. The continued presence of Lenape families posed no threat to Quaker expansion and provided an easy opportunity to practice charity and kindness. The Webbs, Harlans, Pierces, and Marshalls did not register any legal complaints at the county or provincial level to legally force these Lenape families from the contested lands because they were confident that it was only a matter of time before the last of the Lenapes disappeared from southeastern Pennsylvania.

Neither Hannah nor Freeman is a Lenape name. There is no evidence to explain how she acquired these names. The naming of a Lenape child is a ceremony that takes place well after birth, and on some occasions a Lenape girl or boy may have more than one name bestowed upon them in their lifetime. There were also names for public use as well as those used for ceremony and so not commonly shared.[5] The surname Freeman has several possible explanations. One of the easiest is an explanation similar to the one often used to explain how former African slaves acquired English surnames: either the name was assigned to them by slave owners or they chose it after being freed. In the case of eighteenth-century Native Americans, occasionally English names were acquired in the process of conversion to Christianity or were chosen to commemorate a relationship to someone they honored or worked for. But Hannah Freeman never converted to Christianity, and she had no work or land relationship to anyone named Freeman in the area. In southeastern Pennsylvania the Freeman name was often associated with free blacks who had moved north into Pennsylvania, finding Quaker sentiments on abolition an attractive factor, but nothing in Hannah's history places her in a close relationship with black freedmen in the area.[6]

While there is no convincing explanation for her surname, there is more to say about her given name. Hannah is an English name with biblical origins and was extremely common among Chester County's eighteenth-century Quaker inhabitants. The pool of first names used during this era is extremely limited, and Hannah was assuredly one of the most popular. Curiously, in the Lenape language Hannah translates to "river," usually used in conjunction with another descriptor. For example, Susquehanna means "muddy river." Various spellings abound—*hane, hanne, hone*—but the pronunciation of the English and Lenape words are nearly identical.[7] Perhaps this was a name Hannah chose or one that she was given to use in her relationships outside her family. The third and most common rendering of her name is Indian Hannah. This name in particular strikes at the heart of the relationship between English colonials and the indigenous peoples they largely dispossessed. Indian Pete, Indian Nellie, and similar generalizations are racially infused nicknames found scattered throughout colonial documentary sources, and their use further complicates the recovery of Indian history in Pennsylvania and elsewhere. Most modern residents of southeastern Pennsylvania continue to easily recognize "Indian Hannah." Such descriptors depersonalize and diminish the autonomy and individuality of those who bore such names. Colonial Pennsylvania scholar Jane Merritt demonstrates that the renaming of Delawares was both a formal and informal process that had multiple meanings and purposes. In many cases renaming people and landscapes was an act that assumes and asserts dominance—a power to determine the identity of people, rivers, and mountains. Assigning a generic name to one's indigenous neighbors was not unlike building fences on lands one did not own. There is a presumption that there would be no contestation and an assumed hierarchy of authority.[8]

Hannah Freeman was born at a critical juncture in her people's history. In the 1720s the Lenape peoples began a mass diaspora out of their historic homelands that would continue for over a century. But if we take into account all the references to the continuing Indian presence in Chester County after their exodus, it appears that many families, like Hannah's, chose not to leave but continued to live in southeastern Pennsylvania. Local records are rife with recollections of Indian settlements of five or six houses, usually located near springs and along streams like Bennett's Run. Many of these settlements had orchards and gardens, suggesting a well-established way of life that tolerated the presence and land claims of the English settlers who surrounded and outnumbered them after the 1720s. Some colonists recalled Indian neighbors who worked beside them in the fields or others who came to collect plant materials for making baskets and other crafts they sold to local merchants and farmers. Still other settlers in the Brandywine River valley remembered friendship and kindness extended by local Lenape neighbors, whether it was providing food to a hungry family, care for settlers' children, or additional labor when the times demanded it. The Lamborn family remembers their father having such good relations with local Lenapes that he would leave his door open, even when he was away from home, so they could take shelter during their travels. His kindness was repaid by gifts of food and friendship. Indians were everywhere in southeastern Pennsylvania long after the greater part of their population began their diaspora west. However, few of these person-to-person, day in and day out transactions find their way into the official colonial records. In the decades following Hannah's birth, there is no evidence suggesting that anyone attempted to move these Indian families or legally challenged their right to live and work throughout the region. In particular, everyone kept whatever negotiations, agreements, and disputes that may have occurred between Hannah and her neighbors off the record until Hannah Freeman grew old.

Hannah Freeman worked all of her life. Like her Quaker counterpart Hannah Marshall, she began her day knowing her responsibilities to her family and her community. She filled each day with the chores and duties she had learned as a young girl from the Lenape women with whom she spent most of her childhood. She received daily instructions not only from immediate family members but also from the network of extended kin who were now dispersed throughout a region that extended beyond the colonial boundaries of Pennsylvania into New Jersey and Delaware. When it came time for Hannah to learn how to plant corn, she did not have just one instructor, she had many. When it was time for her to learn how to bake, to mend a fishing net, or to mix the paints for her baskets, she listened to and watched a group of women whose accumulated knowledge was built on generations of experience and tradition.

Hannah's immediate family consisted of her grandmother Jane, maternal aunts Betty and Nanny, her father, and her mother, Sarah.[9] She had two brothers, both younger than herself, who were also born along Bennett's Run. Nothing is known about Hannah's brothers or what became of them in later decades, but it is clear from her earliest recollections that her immediate family and the family that would remain her closest circle all of her life was woman centered. Describing this in the basic anthropological term of "matrilineal" has its problems and flattens out details that are important to Hannah's story. The community of women Hannah knew had a foundation based in both tradition and change. It included some of her maternal kin, as Lenape tradition dictated, but it was also a community shaped and formed both by the influx of various refugee Indian groups who passed through Pennsylvania during this tumultuous period and by the Quaker women who were her lifelong neighbors. Hannah was born to the Turtle Clan of the Brandywine Lenape at a time when the political and economic structure of the society that her mother and grandmothers had known had collapsed due to the diaspora of her people. Hannah and other Indian women like her would find new ways to live in this changing and challenging world. Her story is so important because it is a story of success and change, not loss and disappearance. Hannah Freeman remained true to her Lenape identity and was extremely successful at resisting domination and total acculturation by her European neighbors. She remained a Lenape woman all of her life and never abandoned her beloved river valley, but being Lenape in that place and that time was unlike the experiences of those who had gone before her.[10]

From her Lenape kin Hannah learned how to sustain herself and her family from the land. In that community work and responsibilities were clearly divided along gendered lines. In the seventeenth and eighteenth century Lenape women were the horticulturalists. The single most important work of the community was the production of food, and it involved everyone in a Lenape neighborhood. While both men and women provided the labor necessary in the production of food, Lenape women working in groups provided leadership in the production of maize and other agricultural commodities. Similarly, although Lenape women assisted in hunting and fishing, Lenape men directed and oversaw these seasonal activities. If we consider "land ownership" in Lenape society as being responsible for land management and use, then Lenape women like Hannah, Sarah, Jane, and Nanny were in a position of "ownership" equivalent to the Quaker men. It is not important to apply any strict gender division in the Lenapes' relationship to the administration of their responsibilities. The divisions were not rigid and unchanging. In fact, faced with the monumental changes introduced by the western European settlers, the Lenapes excelled at adapting to the new opportunities and obstacles these encounters presented. The relationships between indigenous men and women and their respective roles in their societies continue to be one of the most misunderstood aspects of these early encounters.[11]

European men, authors of most early observations of Indian men and women, were constrained by their own mores and customs and thus regularly misinterpreted what they observed. Early English chroniclers of indigenous Americans John Smith and Roger Williams saw Indian women as little more than slaves. Smith observed that "the women be verie painefulle and the men often idle." Williams concurred, considering the Indian women under undue force and labor when they worked in the fields.[12] When Lenape women planted, tended, and harvested their gardens, European men saw their labor as coerced enslavement because they thought they were performing men's duties. When the settlers saw Lenape men leave their homes for months at a time to hunt or fish, English colonists believed they were participating in a sport meant only for the leisure class and abandoning their responsibilities. English colonists were therefore incapable of giving an accurate account of a way of life they did not understand. But although this was unseen by English eyes, the Lenapes lived in a fairly egalitarian society. There was no hierarchical structure dividing the society either on the basis of wealth or of sex roles. Further, the relationships between Lenape men and women are best described as complementary. The power and authority of men and women rested in their contributions to the well-being of their community, and everyone shared those responsibilities. And while the Lenapes, like so many others, would face an assault on their societies in the decades after colonization, the very essence of Lenape identity remained intact. Hannah Freeman learned what was expected from her as a woman in Lenape society from generations of older Lenape women. She learned through observation, through lessons and stories, and through experience. These learned traditions and obligations were not barriers that inhibited or limited her future; rather, they proved to be the foundation of her successful transformation during this century of change and turmoil.

"This story makes camp."[13] It is easy to imagine Hannah as a young girl sitting on a well-worn woven mat in her family's cabin as her grandmother opened a story with this traditional saying. The Lenapes understood the story as a living entity that came to life through the storyteller. When the storyteller began to speak, the story came into the house and made camp. When the storyteller stopped speaking, the living story departed until called upon again. Every story had a lesson to teach, something to know and remember. Many stories were told at particular times of year and not spoken any other time. Some stories were told only by women passing on knowledge that belonged to them. Some stories were told to a selected few who were destined to carry on special gifts and responsibilities for their people, like sachems or healers. As a young girl Hannah began the process of acquiring the generations-old accumulated knowledge of her people. The first stories she heard as a child sitting around the family hearth instructed young Hannah about her place in the Lenape community and her place in the universe.

One of the earliest stories she might have heard from her grandmother relates an account of the Lenape people and their long journey to find their homeland. According to some traditions the Lenape peoples traveled from some distance in search of a homeland where they could live in peace. It was a story that spoke of the strength of her people, but it also imbedded an understanding that the Lenape home was where the Lenape lived. This lesson would serve well the generations who experienced the diaspora.[14] There were other aspects of Hannah's ceremonial life that might have strengthened her understanding of change and transformation. Imbedded in annual ritual observance of the new harvest or the ceremonies of universal renewal later identified as the Big House religion, Lenapes understood transformation and change as part of their worldview.[15]

There were other stories that taught Hannah her role as a daughter, sister, wife, mother, and grandmother. Hannah listened to stories of the creator, *Kishelemukong*, forming the earth out of mud on Grandfather Turtle's back. *Kishelemukong* gave life to other sacred entities, all members of a sacred family. The sun and thunder are elder brothers, corn is the mother, three of the four directions are grandfathers, and the south is grandmother. A spiritual force, *Manetuwak*, infuses all life on Turtle Island: animals, astronomical phenomenon, even weather. *Kishelemukong* created a first man and first woman from whom all Lenape are descended out of the trees that emerged on Turtle Island.[16] The stories of Corn Mother are especially important to Lenape women. Corn Mother taught Hannah that the success or failure of her people, their very survival and place in the universe, depended on her actions and the fulfillment of her obligations. Hannah shared this responsibility with her community, but each individual was accountable for his or her actions in relationship with the sacred world. Corn Mother is an elder.

The Peaceable Kingdom

She holds dominion over the gardens and orchards, the source of foods that sustained Hannah's people. There were ceremonial obligations to honor Corn Mother that were essential to the success or failure of a harvest, the bounty or starvation of her people. Corn Mother demanded much of the Lenape people, but she was generous and forgiving of their mistakes. Hannah and her sister kin understood their central role in the future of their people. As a little girl Hannah probably had a corn doll made of husks, passed down through her family, that helped to teach her the meaning of her obligations. Most likely she attended the annual ceremonies that honored the first planting and the harvest. Women were instrumental in the rituals and dressed in special clothing and adornment as they both expressed the role of Corn Mother and honored her sacredness during the first planting.[17]

Hannah Marshall and other Quaker girls shared a set of moral and spiritual obligations that shaped their daily lives as well. She too learned her place in her family from her mother and father. She learned the moral principals of the Society of Friends from the members of the meeting that her parents attended and no doubt learned to read from the Quaker texts and lessons that were published in Philadelphia and readily available to Chester County's Quakers. Both girls grew up in a world where peace and generosity were honored over violence and selfishness, although the latter remained threatening aspects of their daily lives. At the core of Lenape ethics is reciprocity. Europeans who first met with Lenapes recognized this cultural aspect and repeatedly witnessed it in the ceremonies, trade relationships, and alliances they shared. As for the Quakers, the very existence and success of Penn's original enterprise rested on a doctrinal commitment to the Peace Testimony and a desire for harmonious coexistence.[18] While Hannah Freeman and Hannah Marshall shared an understanding of the importance of peace, kindness, and generosity, Hannah Freeman looked out on a landscape alive with visible and invisible spirits, both negative and positive. Her spiritual world was rich with rituals, ceremonies, and dreams that helped her and her people maintain balance throughout the whole universe.[19] Hannah Marshall and the other Quaker women Hannah Freeman would come to know as friends and neighbors did not know that spiritually enlivened natural world. Instead they lived in a society that was nearly void of ceremony and ritual but shaped by a demand for adherence to procedures and practices that proscribed their daily lives. On many levels the Quakers and Lenapes living in the Brandywine River Valley in the early eighteenth century had more in common than is typically perceived. But the possibility of this tenuous stability lasting long was shattered by the voracious demands of Pennsylvania's colonial expansion.

Hannah's world changed rapidly as Quaker settlements surrounded and eventually isolated her extended family from other enclaves of Lenape families in the region. Her family members' subsistence remained centered on the cultivation of their gardens, but changes in the land and access to previous resources altered both their diet and their work. However, these changes also offered new opportunities and experiences that would become part of Hannah's life as she grew to adulthood along the Brandywine River. Lenape corn cultivation changed little during those decades. While the size of Lenape gardens and fields decreased, the fertile river bottomlands continued to easily produce an abundant crop of corn. She and her family also enjoyed the freedom to move seasonally between two or more homesteads but experienced limitations in where they could travel, what lands were open to their gathering of plants, and access to ceremonial sites. Even access to the graves of their relatives became more difficult. Quakers looked on new fences, bridges, and roads as signs of progress and prosperity. Hannah's family probably experienced these signs of progress with uncertainty and some contempt. Nevertheless, Hannah Freeman and other Lenapes who chose to stay in their ancient homeland learned

The Peaceable Kingdom

to embrace the changes and showed great resilience by making the best life they could in this new century.

In the winter Hannah and her family lived in their cabin on Bennett's Run and in the late spring and summer they moved to their lands a little further up the river, where they planted their gardens on the more open expanses of their cleared fields.[20] Spring was a busy time for Lenape and Quaker farmers alike. The most important activity was preparing the fields for planting. Lenape women organized their work and determined the right time to plant seeds based on their astronomical knowledge and understanding of the seasons. They observed changes in the soil and other factors that informed their decisions about where to plant and when. Smaller family groups undoubtedly required that everyone work to get the fields planted, a change in work patterns that was more like their colonial neighbors. Young and old, male and female—all were all needed in these new community configurations, but women provided the leadership and expertise as they had for generations. Hannah followed her mother into the fields and learned along the way, imitating her mother's work. Eventually she acquired the skills and experience that allowed her to work independently.

Hannah's family did not live on corn alone; pumpkins and beans were planted in their gardens as well. Corn, beans, and squash are known to many indigenous North Americans as the "three sisters" because they grew together in the fields, with the corn providing the stock for the beans to entwine, while the squash provided a ground cover that preserved the soil's moisture and discouraged weeds. These three foods made a nearly perfect nutritional combination, with meat and fish only supplementing this staple diet. Hannah Freeman also learned how to cultivate orchards and berry patches that added variation and pleasure to their daily meals.[21] This part of their agricultural activity was not foraging, a term often used to delineate the work of indigenous farmers from their "civilized" colonial neighbors. Much knowledge, planning, and skillful manipulation went into the Lenapes' horticultural work.

Not all the plants gathered and cultivated by Hannah and her family were for food. Lenape women were known for their fine weaving of plant fibers; they turned raw materials into thread and yarn that was woven into clothing, mats, bags, fishing nets, and a variety of other useful objects. Hemp grew along the bottomlands as well as reeds and grasses, and these were woven into baskets. The seasons dictated when these plants would be harvested, and ceremonies and prayers accompanied many of these activities. Though Hannah's family wore clothing made largely from cotton and flax like their Quaker neighbors, Lenape textiles and baskets were unmatched and continued to find a market in colonial settlements throughout the eighteenth century.[22]

Turning plant fibers into thread and yarn involved an array of skills that would prove to be extremely valuable to Hannah Freeman as she grew to adulthood living immersed in the regional Quaker economy. Her baskets and mats provided a small source of income through trade for goods and services, but it was her talents in spinning, sewing, and weaving that resulted in a more reliable income throughout her adult life. Weaving and spinning were ancient arts that Hannah Freeman learned from her relatives. Early Dutch settlers were regular customers for the craftwork produced by Lenape women. They were especially fascinated with the Indians' method of producing yarn. The women harvested hemp and other plant fibers, turning the prepared raw materials into strong and pliable yarn by rolling the materials back and forth across their thighs. Moistening and twisting the fibers gave them strength and elasticity. Like cotton and flax fibers, hemp could be manipulated into varying degrees of coarseness for everything from rope to fishing line, storage baskets to purses.

Hannah's textile skills provided her with an opportunity to transition from the now vulnerable subsistence economy her extended family relied on and facilitated her entry into the world of wage labor, an important detail Moses Marshall included in his "Examination." Chester County's first economic success

The Peaceable Kingdom

was the result of its agricultural productivity. Penn's colony was often identified as the "breadbasket" of the thirteen colonies. But farming had seasonal rounds that created fluctuating demands for labor. Planting and harvesting required many workers, while winter months demanded fewer. Furthermore, the growing number of settlers in the rural counties increased the demands for goods from Philadelphia and beyond. Chester County's burgeoning population necessitated the development of a local economy that mixed agriculture with local craftwork and home-based manufacturing. Laborers worked for payment in local products and in wages that they used to buy goods from distant markets. The production of cloth from flax became an important local labor activity and source of income; Hannah Freeman's skills and knowledge were marketable commodities.

In colonial southeastern Pennsylvania fabric represented the largest expenditure in the average household budget. Fabric was needed not only for clothing but also for household and agricultural purposes. Chester County families demanded hundreds of yards of cloth for shirts, aprons, sheets, curtains, winnowing cloths, feed sacks, and so much more. The majority of cloth in Chester County was produced from flax, with cotton and hemp in much less demand. By midcentury flax seed was one of Pennsylvania's most important export commodities, with the majority going to Ireland's markets, where it furnished the raw material for production of the famous Irish linen. Producing fabric from flax was a labor- and resource-intensive enterprise that complemented the seasonal fluctuations of agricultural labor. Hannah's involvement in the activity gave her access to the growing cash-based economy and the material world of her Quaker coworkers.[23]

The various stages of cloth production, from planting to weaving, were divided along gender lines. Flax planting began in the spring; it was harvested in midsummer. More women than men worked in the fields because pulling flax doesn't demand the use of scythes as the harvesting of rye and wheat does. The job required little skill, but it was an easy opportunity for Hannah and other Lenape women to earn wages or goods. Once pulled, the flax was spread on the fields to "ret" the stalks, making it easier to separate the long and short plant fibers. By winter the plant fibers were ready to be carded and spun into yarn, a task that required specialized skills and was performed almost exclusively by women. Hannah Marshall and other young Quaker girls learned spinning from their mothers as young as five years old. They learned how to spin flax the same way Hannah Freeman learned to spin hemp, by watching and imitating their mothers and grandmothers. By the time girls were adolescents they were apprentices of the trade and many entered Chester County's female workforce. It may be that Hannah Freeman, befriended by her neighbors, sat next to young Quaker women and learned how to use a spinning wheel, twisting the long silky fibers into thread. It is easy to imagine Hannah working with a small group of Quaker women, keeping time with the treadle, producing thread much faster than her grandmother ever could. It is more difficult to picture how Hannah fit into this scene during the long winter months when this work was done. The women, daughters and widows who sought this seasonal work, most often brought their personal belongings with them and stayed in their employer's household for periods of days and sometimes weeks until the job was done. Their employer deducted room, board, and supplies from their wages, which he paid in cash, goods, or a combination of the two.[24] Hannah earned comparable wages and goods for her work: on average she earned a shilling a day.[25] But did Hannah find friendship in these small circles of laboring women or was she treated differently, working separately from the others? By the mid-eighteenth century, Quaker women understood Lenapes to be deserving of pity and sympathy, worthy of their charity and in need of civilizing. Certainly Hannah's dark skin, strange language, and social manners separated her from these women in stark ways. But it is also possible to imagine that the women laughed together and helped each other in their common work. Historian Laurel Thatcher Ulrich points out that the sort of home textile production that Hannah and her Quaker neighbors participated in was more than an economic activity—it also represented social relationships.[26] As Hannah grew to adulthood she spent more time in close contact with Quaker women than her mother and grandmothers ever had in their lifetimes. She learned many things from the circle of Quaker women she came to know and put much of that knowledge to good use in providing for her family. It is unlikely, however, that this exchange of knowledge and skills was reciprocal. English Quakers in southeastern Pennsylvania were certain of their intellectual and cultural superiority over their Indian neighbors. It is unlikely that Hannah's Quaker coworkers understood who Hannah Freeman was within her own community or her status and authority as one of Turtle Island's daughters. Eventually, however, they would come to learn that Hannah Freeman had some specialized skills and knowledge they would come to value.

Hannah Freeman's English neighbors failed to see many things about her that were in plain sight. From her childhood to later in life she applied a variety of acquired knowledge and skills that were part of the traditional Lenape world to the changing circumstances of her life embedded in a colonial settlement. Beyond the practical daily skills needed as a member of a farming community, Hannah had unique talents that made her someone special and out of the ordinary to both Lenapes and settlers. Hannah Freeman was a doctor. And it was in this capacity that she was indispensable to some of her neighbors. Hannah was the keeper of a body of pharmacological and ethnobotanical knowledge acquired by generations of Lenape elders. Her medical training was not a vocation of choice, but rather a gift bestowed by the spirit world. Early in her life it is likely Hannah Freeman had a dream vision that shaped her future role as a member of her Lenape community and was surely instrumental in determining her destiny as a Lenape woman living in colonial Pennsylvania. She may have had a significant encounter with some aspect of the natural world that spoke to her and identified her as empowered to receive this knowledge. Select Lenapes received such powers from spiritual guides or helpers, who appeared in both human and animal form. Perhaps Hannah had a vision or dream that informed her that she had a special destiny and gift. Once this was known, her family most likely sought out elders in her extended community who could assist in identifying and interpreting the significance of the event. However Hannah Freeman became aware of the path unfolding in front of her as a culture keeper and healer for her people, it is most likely it happened early in her life.[27]

Once Hannah was identified as a potential doctor and healer in her community she probably began to receive instruction in the Lenape medical arts from a more experienced practitioner. It is possible that this mentor was an older woman in her family, as the gift of healing was often handed down through the female line, or it may have been someone outside of her immediate family circle. Her apprenticeship was no small undertaking; it suggests that Hannah was not only a very bright young woman but also one of deep convictions. To be a skilled doctor among her people involved a long and arduous process requiring commitment on many different levels beginning at a young age. Hannah Freeman not only made this commitment to herself, her family, and her community, she did this in the absence of the broader social network that the generations before her had known. Her success in practicing traditional Lenape medicine demanded her absolute faith in the constant power and benevolence of the unseen spirit world. Every facet of Lenape healing arts required appeals and prayers to spiritual forces, which she relied on in her professional practices. In turn, this assurance of the spirit world working in all aspects of her life imbued her with the confidence to face adversity and change with fearlessness. It is imperative to remember that her work was carried out during a period of instability and great

The Peaceable Kingdom

loss for the Lenapes living in southeastern Pennsylvania. It is further evidence there was more to Hannah Freeman than her neighbors fully recognized or appreciated.

In Lenape culture there were two types of healers, and both men and women were practitioners, although most were women. Most of the healing arts practiced by the Lenapes were founded in a knowledge of plant-based remedies and applications. The second category of practices was the province of those who claimed supernatural powers and the ability to affect human actions. Colonists had some respect for the first type of Lenape healers, taking note of "the good and honest practitioners who are in the habit of curing and healing diseases by the simple application of natural remedies." But they observed with disdain the "sorcerers . . . who pretend to be skilled in a certain occult science" and claimed the power to "expel evil spirits."[28]

Eighteenth-century colonial medical practices had much in common with Hannah's traditional knowledge. Both Lenape and English healers relied heavily on a botanically based medicine cabinet to cure the illnesses and maladies of their patients. Despite claims of intellectual and cultural superiority, colonial Americans and the broader scientific community had no deeper understanding of the causes of disease than did their indigenous counterparts. Perhaps the greatest difference between the healing arts of the two cultures was that western Europeans and American colonists generally believed that illnesses were caused by an imbalance of the four humors in the human body. When these four substances were in balance, one enjoyed good health. But when they were not, any and all diseases could be traced to the imbalance. One of the most common practices of eighteenth-century doctors was to rectify the imbalance by bleeding the patient. Essentially, colonial doctors used unsterilized tools to cut into the vein of an ill person, allowing blood to drain into a bowl, the idea being that draining the "ill" humors allowed the patient hope of recovery by the body's response. This practice often did more harm than good, further weakening an already ill person. This explanation for the cause of disease was centuries old, originating in Greek antiquity, and it remained common until the nineteenth century. Lenapes also based their explanation for disease and sickness on very ancient ideas. They believed that illness stemmed from an imbalance in one's spiritual well-being, not in ones bodily fluids. Cures for illnesses began with trying to locate and identify the source of the imbalance. Causes could be anything, including failing to keep ceremonies or not living a right life. One could also become ill by encountering unseen malevolent forces. While Hannah and her neighbors understood the root cause of illness differently, they both put their faith in the curative powers of the natural world.[29]

Hannah acquired a great store of knowledge about the medicinal uses of plants and had at her disposal the fields and forests of the Brandywine River valley. The acquisition of leaves, roots, flowers, and seeds was only one aspect of her practice. Ceremony, too, was involved in every aspect of her profession. If Hannah was called upon to heal a neighbor with a fever, she might have made a tea of any number of plants like wild thyme and hops. If it were dysentery, she might have administered pennyroyal and mint. Whatever her prescription for the patient, we can be certain that every aspect of her practice, from obtaining the plant to curing, preserving, and preparing, was accompanied by prayers, rituals, and songs. Hannah's special skills as a doctor suggest she knew rules that governed all aspects of her practice down to the day, time, and season specific to each plant.

Hannah's reputation as a healer extended beyond her own Lenape community. On occasion her Quaker neighbors entrusted the care of their children to Hannah's herbal preparations. Hannah Chalfourt suffered from whooping cough, a respiratory ailment that modern medicine treats through childhood vaccinations. In the eighteenth century it was a disease that could kill both adolescents and adults. The Chalfourts turned to Hannah for her medical expertise. After seeing their daugh-

The Peaceable Kingdom

ter, Hannah Freeman went into the forest and returned with the necessary ingredients to treat the child's illness. Her remedy aided the young girl's return to good health. In another instance Quaker minister John Parker's family suffered from dysentery, which at the time was an epidemic in the region. The intestinal infection, left untreated, was life threatening, especially to children. The origins of the epidemic were unknown, but several deaths were reported in the area. The Quaker father turned to Hannah to return his family to health. She successfully treated the members of his family, and it was said that anyone who drank her "tea" recovered from the illness. Hannah's remedy might have contained sassafras or pine needles, both known as effective treatments. John Parker appreciated and respected Hannah's expertise and returned to her for other remedies, at one point paying her 5 shillings for her prescriptions.[30] Members of the Quaker Kennett Meeting, John Parker's own congregation, must have known about Hannah's doctoring, and many probably followed his lead, hiring her to treat their families on occasion as well.

There was no shortage of expert medical practitioners and scientists in the area who might have been called upon to diagnose and treat local patients. Humphry Marshall and Moses Marshall were well-known botanists whose specimen gardens were famous. They had a particular interest in indigenous plants, an interest shared with their more well-known cousin John Bartram. John Bartram wrote several books on North American plant species and enjoyed international recognition during Hannah's lifetime. Along with Benjamin Franklin, he cofounded the American Philosophical Society in 1747, one of the most important intellectual institutions in the thirteen colonies. Bartram and the Marshalls collected and exchanged information on the indigenous uses of various plants with an international circle of scientists. Bartram traveled from Cherokee and Choctaw lands in the southeast to the Onondaga near the Great Lakes collecting data and plant specimens from his indigenous counterparts and local settlers.[31] It is hard to imagine that part of their intellectual endeavors were not informed by local indigenous knowledge in southeastern Pennsylvania, perhaps including details Hannah Freeman shared with her astute neighbors. Other doctors practiced medicine in the region as well. William Baldwin studied with the Marshalls and later had a professional practice in Wilmington, Delaware. Abraham Bailey practiced medicine in Chester County until 1800.[32] Jacob Pierce, a neighbor along the Brandywine River, provided medical services for Hannah in her later years. Coincidentally or not, the Brandywine River valley and Chester County had their fair share of professionally trained medical and pharmacological experts—but Hannah's services remained in demand with many in the region.

Whether in the course of her work as spinner or as doctor, Hannah Freeman spent much of her time traveling alone along the roads and paths of Chester County. As a Lenape woman, her economic independence was not unusual, but as an Indian woman living behind the volatile and permeable border between Indian country and the colonial backcountry, her solitary travels required greater courage. Early European observers regularly took note of the autonomy and independence of Lenape women. In trade they were often on the front lines negotiating exchanges for the products of their agricultural activities and various trade items the settlers needed. Lenape women, like so many other indigenous women in the Americas, were active participants in the newly emerging global markets, even though their activities often went unnoticed by later historians of the colonial era. Lenape women were known to travel far from their communities, on horseback and on foot, to bring their marketable goods to the towns, ports, and cities. Hannah's mobility throughout the region was remarkable. She walked from farm to farm to work for local farmers who hired her for seasonal labor. She sometimes rode her horse to doctor her neighbors, whose homes were spread far and wide along the Brandywine

River valley. While this mobility was reminiscent of the independence and autonomy of her mother and grandmothers, Hannah Freeman made her solitary way through a landscape that Lenapes no longer controlled. Hannah Freeman spent much of her life passing back and forth through one of the most violent regions in the thirteen colonies.

By midcentury Pennsylvania was far removed from the idealized "peaceable kingdom" William Penn had imagined a half century earlier. This continued characterization of colonial Pennsylvania as an exception to colonial violence elsewhere is not only problematic but runs counter to current scholarship. Violent crime was a critical feature of the society. Homicides and assaults exceeded the number of all other crimes committed in the colony, giving it a unique distinction among the other British colonies in North America: in those colonies property crimes surpassed violent crimes in number throughout the eighteenth century. Pennsylvania's homicide rate in the 1720s alone exceeded London's for all of the eighteenth century. By the time Checochinican led the majority of his people out of the Brandywine River valley, Chester County was the most violent county in the thirteen colonies.[33] Indeed, this may be one reason why Hannah's people decided to forsake their ancestral homeland in favor of putting space between them and the rapidly expanding colonial settlements.

While most scholars cite Quaker morality and pacifism as a major component of the earlier tranquility the colony had enjoyed, the Lenapes' contributions to this early civil society played no small part. Before William Penn's arrival the Delaware River valley was a politically and economically stable region, even with the influx of Swedish, Dutch, and English colonists. Lenape hegemony in the region established relatively peaceful relationships with the new settlers as well as other indigenous groups who sought access to the trade. The "peaceable kingdom" that William Penn envisioned was well under way before he sailed up the Delaware River. The Lenapes, like the Quakers, sought to avoid war and violent confrontations in favor of negotiations, equitable exchanges, and a set of behaviors and customs that were mutually acceptable. William Penn ordered his representatives and agents to treat the Lenapes fairly in all transactions, especially in regard to criminal activity. Early on Penn and Lenape leaders insisted that if crimes were committed against and between their peoples, then justice must prevail on either side, from accusation to apprehension to the implementation of punishment.[34] And for the first four decades of the colony's existence this mutual civility prevailed over more volatile forces such as had shaped the original decades of other colonies, from Massachusetts to Virginia. The pacifist sensibilities of the Society of Friends and the importance of reciprocity in the Lenapes' philosophy prevailed until an influx of new immigrants forced unwanted changes on both populations.

New immigrants and their demands for land in Pennsylvania not only led to the Lenapes' dispossession of their ancestral homeland, they tested every aspect of Penn's principles of tolerance and peaceful coexistence. By midcentury Pennsylvania had the third-largest population in the thirteen colonies. The majority of the new immigrants were either German-speaking Pietists or Scots-Irish settlers from Ulster. The Quaker majority responded to this influx of new people with distrust and skepticism. Leaders of the provincial assembly, anxious about the Germans, in 1727 passed laws that required German immigrants to register with the government and swear oaths of allegiance.[35] Eventually the German immigrants' hard work and modest lifestyle reconciled the English Pennsylvanians to their presence after this initial period of concern. The new Scots-Irish immigrants, however, posed an altogether different danger that did not diminish over time.

The Scots-Irish settlers arrived in Pennsylvania with a reputation as a belligerent and violent people. Theirs was a clan-based culture, and they had spent generations in the shadow of English domination, fighting for control of their ancestral homelands on the borders between England and Scotland. Coming from this contested and militarized landscape, the largely Presbyterian population lived in a world of violence, lawlessness, and contempt for distant authorities. In an effort of bring peace to this war-torn region, the indigenous populations of the Scottish Lowlands were relocated to Northern Ireland as part of the Crown's objective to colonize and control the island's majority Catholic population. The Crown's use of Scots-Irish as frontline colonial shock troops succeeded in dispossessing Irish peasants from their lands while contributing to a race-based hatred that continues to trouble Ireland centuries later. In the first quarter of the eighteenth century the Scots-Irish heirs of English domination and dispossession began to cross the Atlantic to England's colonies, seeking opportunities as freeholders, with Pennsylvania receiving the vast majority of their numbers. Between 1727 and 1730 ten thousand Ulster immigrants arrived in Philadelphia seeking opportunities to finally control their own destiny.[36] The colony's reputation for religious tolerance and its abundant and fertile land beckoned the sons and daughters of Ulster to stake a claim in William Penn's colony.

The influx of immigrants eventually unseated Quaker authority after midcentury, but Penn's heirs and the Quaker elite throughout the settled counties of the colony sought to restrain and manage the influx of settlers in the early years. Many elite English Quakers responded with disgust and concern regarding the number of "foreigners" invading their well-tended colony. But just as much as they openly despised and feared the changes the German and Scots-Irish settlers represented, some of their fellow Quakers saw opportunity. James Logan's initial response to the changing demography of southeastern Pennsylvania was similar to his countrymen's, but before long he used his office as commissioner of property to direct the new settlements to the colony's best advantage. While the majority of German immigrants occupied lands to the north of Philadelphia, Logan channeled the Scots-Irish to the western borderlands along the Susquehanna River. As Logan heard and affirmed Checochinican's claims against unlawful English settlement on Lenape lands along the Brandywine River, he also turned a blind eye to the unlawful squatting of Ulster settlers on Indian lands in the western backcountry. In effect he used both of these immigrant groups to expand the colony's boundaries, dispossess Indians from their lands, and reap revenues from their sweat and muscle. As Logan and other elite Quakers governed, legislated, and pontificated about the undesirable qualities of the "swarms" of outsiders descending upon the "peaceable kingdom," the crime, poverty, and increased anti-Indian sentiments turned the former Lenape homelands into a landscape fraught with potential risks.

Hannah Freeman and other Indian women traversed a countryside that was rife with danger. As she crossed the paths and roads of the county she may have walked and talked with the transient poor who passed through the country looking for work and opportunity. Perhaps she worked alongside these nameless women in the harvesting and spinning of flax, or perhaps she tended sick children in the small tenant cabins scattered on the larger Quaker plantations. Chester County claimed a proportionally high number of people on the move who had neither permanent residence nor employment in the region. The largely agricultural economy attracted seasonal workers, and the associated temporary housing brought tenants and renters. One study noted that Pennsylvania had a "subterranean river of people" flowing through Chester County.[37] The increased number of violent crimes in the county can be partially attributed to both the anonymity and desperate poverty of this portion of the population. But not all crimes were reported, and court statistics tell us little about violent crimes committed against the Indian people living in Chester County.

Hannah Freeman and other Indian people seemed to live in a sort of quasi-legal space during this period of colonial expansion. On one hand, because the Brandywine Lenape were members of a known Indian community, issues regarding crimes committed by or against members of Checochinican's peoples would have fallen to the Lenape leadership to settle, either in association with the colonial government or internally. But the only protections or recourses of individual Indian peoples and families outside of local Lenape judicial authority were colonial criminal codes and the authority of thinly spread sheriffs and justices of the peace. Concurrent with the Lenapes' uncertain legal status in the county was the intensified hostility broadly directed at any and all Indians. The Scots-Irish had a particularly virulent hatred of the Indian peoples directly related to their haphazard settlement, both legal and not, in the backcountry borders of Pennsylvania. The Ulster settlers' animosity was fueled by their distrust of the elite Quakers governing from distant Philadelphia and their proximity to Indian country beyond the Susquehanna River. The newly created Lancaster County carved out of larger Chester County, home to the majority of these new settlers, was beyond the reach of Pennsylvania's authority. Much of the governance and leadership of these backcountry communities fell into the hands of their own Presbyterian ministers, who not only joined them in their anti-Quaker and Indian-hating sentiments but often gave legitimacy to their cause. Within decades the many-faceted hostilities, fueled by provincial neglect and boundary disputes in the backcountry, would erupt into war.

Before the outbreak of the French and Indian War in 1754, crimes against Indians were largely unreported. The documented enumerations of homicides, assaults, and other violent crimes represent only those cases that made it to the courts. Crimes against more vulnerable members of the community are harder to identify and understand. The very survival of isolated individual Indians and their families who chose to stay on their homelands behind the borders of colonial expansion depended on some level of secrecy and invisibility. It is unlikely that individual Lenapes would come forward to report crimes against their persons or property, for to make complaints would lead to interaction with colonial authorities. It is easy to imagine that Indian people fell victim to a variety of crimes committed by a transient population who resented them based on either real or imagined transgressions. But on occasion there were crimes committed against local Indians that were so heinous they could not be ignored by colonial authorities. And for Hannah Freeman, one such incident fell very close to home.

Most of the perpetrators of violent crimes reported in Chester County in the eighteenth century were men, and the majority of victims were women. Rape in particular was perhaps one of the most underreported violent crimes against women; historians Jack Marietta and G. S. Rowe aptly characterize it as the "most serious case of the dark figures of crime" in the colony.[38] The "dark figures" are crimes that go unreported, unprosecuted, and hidden from enumeration. Between 1682 and 1800 only fifty-seven prosecutions for rape appear on the record. Women did not report the crime because they were not treated fairly in the judicial system. When race is factored into this reticence, then it is easy to assume that black and Indian women had almost no chance of receiving a fair response to rape accusations. Despite these odds, an Indian woman known only as Betty broke through this barrier of "dark figures" in the Chester County courts.

On August 13, 1722, James Brown attacked Betty behind a barn in Kennett Township. The Browns were prominent Quaker landowners in the Brandywine River valley; their lands had been parceled from the same grants that provided the Marshalls, Harlans, Barnards, and Pierces their homesteads along the river. There is little to identify Betty other than her Indian identity, but it is worth noting that Hannah's aunt was named Betty and lived in the same neighborhood in which the crime took place. Was there more than one local Indian woman known as Betty to her Quaker neighbors, or was this Hannah's aunt? We cannot know with any certainty the particulars of her relation-

The Peaceable Kingdom

ship with Hannah, but within a Lenape frame of reference, they were family because they were Lenapes, and the violent nature of the crime must have had an impact on those who knew Betty. How this particular crime made its way into the courts when countless other did not is uncertain, but the evidence presented against James Brown left little doubt of his guilt. Numerous depositions by witnesses who found Betty in the aftermath of the attack as well as by those who heard Brown's own admissions of guilt testified that he threw her to the ground and "then and there did beat and wound and evilly entreat so that of her life it was greatly despaired."[39] Witnesses found Betty burned and beaten, unable to rise from the ground.

The depositions come very close to describing what appears to be a sexual assault, but Brown was not accused of rape. Witnesses described Betty with her skirts pulled above her head, leaving little doubt of the nature of the crime. The incident must have been shocking to the Quakers who knew the Browns through business transactions or in attendance at Sunday services together. With all the cultural and social barriers that suppressed not only violence in this quiet Quaker community but sexual relations with an Indian woman as well, how do we come to terms with such a violent and personal attack on a familiar Lenape neighbor? However we come to understand this event, Chester County indicted James Brown and, despite his claims of innocence, the Court of Quarter Sessions found him guilty of assault.[40] Perhaps the reason Brown was not accused of raping Betty is because as a rapist, Brown would have faced a severe set of statues that reflected the Quakers' changing attitudes about crime and punishment. In 1718 the provincial assembly enacted a harsher criminal code that approved use of the death penalty in the colony, listing rape as a capital offense.[41] Instead the court found Brown guilty of a deadly assault that nearly killed Betty and fined him 20 shillings and the expense of court fees. What behind-the-scenes machinations saved James Brown from being accused of a more serious crime and possibly receiving the death penalty? Was it because of who he was, a member of a prominent Quaker family, or was it because his victim was an Indian woman?

Twenty shillings is an intriguing sum to consider. As stated earlier, at midcentury Hannah Freeman and other women who worked for local landowners like the Browns earned approximately 1 shilling a day for their labor. Brown's fine was not out of the ordinary; in fact the majority of assault convictions resulted in no jail time and fines that were less than 20 shillings (1 pound). What makes the case against Brown stand out is the fact that he denied the accusation and entered a not-guilty plea to the court. Colonial Pennsylvanians committed assault more than any other crime, and it was also the crime least likely to find its way to trial. Grand jurors were less likely to indict one of their citizens for assault than for any other offense. If indicted, the accused could either confess or submit to the court without confessing and face a punishment, pay a fine, and be done with the court. While colonial authorities hoped that capital punishment might deter murder and rape, their response to other violent crimes seems to suggest they were becoming accustomed to physical brutality and aggressive behavior as a part of everyday life. As historians Marietta and Rowe aptly put it, colonial "Pennsylvanians trivialized violence, and thereby encouraged it."[12] This case is an anomaly in that James Brown fought the indictment, his victim was an Indian woman, and the court found him guilty. It is also unique in that numerous witnesses were willing to come forward and give depositions that convinced the court to find Brown guilty. But it is not an anomaly within this context that violent crime was increasingly a real threat to everyone living in colonial Pennsylvania. A fine of 20 shillings did little to assure Hannah Freeman and other Lenape women and men, whose work often found them in isolated and vulnerable situations, that their well-being and safety was important to the colony's jurists.

By midcentury William Penn's dream of a peaceable kingdom

was a lost cause. Penn's haven for religious tolerance and good governance unraveled under the forces of rapid expansion and colonialism. As the elite Quakers in the assembly struggled to regulate settlement and maintain order closer to home, they lost control of the backcountry. Aggressive border disputes and heightened anti-Indian sentiment emboldened the Scots-Irish settlers in their complaints to the governor and assembly. Illegal squatters moved on to lands without regard for the Indian owners, who found themselves embattled in their own country. The long-reaching tentacles of imperial disputes were having an impact on the everyday lives of Native American men and women who tenaciously refused to leave their homelands in Pennsylvania for the temporary safety of lands further north and west. Hannah Freeman and her kin made their way across a familiar landscape, risking their safety and security, in order to remain an independent and free people on their ancestral homelands in Chester County. Some, like Betty, would pay an all too terrible price for that choice. Hannah Freeman's greatest trials were just beginning. As increased violence became an intimate threat within her local community, international conflicts reached deep into southeastern Pennsylvania and tore Hannah's family apart.

CHAPTER FOUR

Lenapehoking Lost

When Hannah Freeman was a young woman, her father "went to Shamokin and never returned." As she recounted her life story to Moses Marshall in 1797, she offered little explanation except that he left at a time when "the country becoming more settled the Indians were not allowed to plant corn any longer."[1] In this brief deposition she offers no explanation for what happened to her father, nor his reasons for the journey. It would be easy to dismiss this episode of her life story in light of an absence of details, except that it marked an abrupt change in how Hannah Freeman and her family conducted their lives. It also came at a time when the relationships between Pennsylvania's provincial government and the Indian peoples living within the colony's claimed boundaries were disintegrating at an unparalleled rate. The departure of Hannah's father was an intimate and personal event that she and her family experienced as the loss of a father, a protector, and a provider for their extended family. But that is only part of the story. Her father's departure to Shamokin connects Hannah and her family to a maelstrom of political goings-on that culminated in an international war that left no one living in the colony untouched. Growth and expansion brought violence and uncertainty into the daily lives of Indian peoples behind the frontier boundaries of the rapidly expanding colony, as was discussed in the previous chapter, and as her father departed for Shamokin, he traveled a well-worn trail that would tie his family to some of the most critical events in the history of colonial North America.

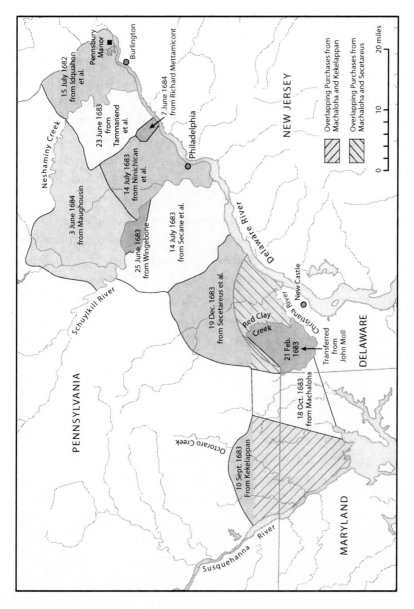

Map 3. Colonial Pennsylvania land cessions.

Shamokin was many things to many people. It was the largest Indian town in Pennsylvania in the mid-eighteenth century, a center of trade and diplomacy and the epicenter of Indian communication routes. The town was founded early in the eighteenth century, most likely by Lenapes, who named the town Shumokenk after the abundance of deer antlers found in the area. The town was situated at the forks of the northern and western branch of the Susquehanna River, and travelers to the town remembered a series of interconnected settlements located on the eastern and western sides of the river's north branch and also on a large island sitting midstream. It is unknown whether or not the town was founded on earlier settlements, but it is easy to understand why the Lenapes would find it a favorable place to settle after 1720. Pennsylvania's immigrant population was exploding, and many Indian people found their ability to hunt, fish, and plant their gardens hampered by the fences, dams, and livestock that the Europeans settlers introduced to the region, just as Hannah recalled. As in the example set by the Brandywine Lenapes' sachem Checochinican, the Lenapes' complaints did little to alter the changes colonization brought to the land and the impact of colonial settlements on Lenape resources. Lenape hunting parties were compelled to travel further north and west in order to satisfy the needs of their communities. Fish camps were abandoned on the southern reaches of the rivers as tributary streams because gristmills and dams prevented the shad from making their way upstream.

Shamokin offered many advantages to Lenapes seeking to put distance between their families and the colonial expansion that impaired their way of life. The town's greatest natural advantage was its location at the confluence of the north and west branches of the Susquehanna River. The northern branch reaches deep into upstate New York, the homelands of the Iroquois. The western branch crosses the Appalachian Mountains and by portages provided the Lenapes with access to western lands, including the Ohio River valley they would soon call home. The broad, muddy river is an ancient system, even older than the mountains it dissects in its southern course to the Chesapeake Bay. The river provided a vital channel of trade, communication, and migration for millennia before the first English stood on its banks. The Lenapes probably had many stories about the river that are now lost to the past: stories of creation, heroic deeds, ancient elders, and the spirit world. Rivers are central to Lenape identity and culture, and the Susquehanna must have loomed large in their history.

Shamokin is also aptly identified as a crossroads, both literally and metaphorically.[2] Indian paths and trails, the origin of many of Pennsylvania's modern highways, easily testify to Shamokin's importance to Indians and immigrants alike. In the eighteenth century all roads in the colony led to Shamokin, either directly or indirectly. Tuscarorans, kin of the Iroquois, abandoned their southern homes in the Carolinas and followed their namesake trail to Shamokin after colonial wars forced them to return to their ancient homelands in the north. There they joined the Great Warriors Path, perhaps the most important of these ancient thoroughfares, a road that followed the northern branch of the Susquehanna River deep into Iroquoia. Members of the Mohawk, Seneca, Oneida, Onondaga, and Cayuga nations traveled this road in times of war and peace, passing through Shamokin so frequently that they eventually claimed the region as their own. The Great Shamokin Path was a vital east-west link that the Brandywine and other Lenape communities traveled as they sought new homes and safe havens west of the Appalachian Mountains. The path ended just north of present-day Pittsburgh, at Kittanning, one of the last major Delaware towns in Pennsylvania. Along with these major roads, smaller paths carried people, news, and goods to Shamokin, making the town a vital link in a complicated network of human interaction; therefore it is not surprising that it played some part in Hannah Freeman's life. Hannah's father probably began his final trip north along the Great Minquas Path that connected

Philadelphia to the Susquehanna River, crossing the Brandywine just a few miles north of his home. From there he probably walked his horse much of the way, skirting the eastern bank
of the river to reach Shamokin. Despite the patchwork of roads
and paths that made Shamokin the terminus of many journeys,
the course was not an easy one.[3] Treacherous mountain crossings and a river that was unpredictable in its current and depth
made a trip to Shamokin arduous no matter the season.

A journey to Shamokin could mean many things. In the mid-
eighteenth century Shamokin was not only familiar to a myriad of Indian peoples, it was also well known to missionaries,
traders, colonial agents, and settlers. In most instances, non-
Indian accounts describe Shamokin as a vortex of diplomatic, spiritual, economic, and social exchange colonists did not
control. Power and authority among the diverse Indian peoples who called it home were regularly challenged by outsiders, whether Shamokin was a temporary or permanent home.
Delaware founders shared the space with numerous Indian
communities which, like themselves, were being dispossessed
of their long-settled lands by colonial habitation. Many people
were moving through or into Pennsylvania during this period,
including the Shawnees, Conoys, Tutelos, Nanticokes, and the
six nations of the Iroquois Confederacy. Moravians, frequent
observers of the town's activities, included Martin and Anne
Mack, who made some attempt to establish a mission in Shamokin. Moravian leader Count Nikolaus Ludwig von Zinzendorf
even paid the town a very brief visit not long after Presbyterian minister David Brainerd was introduced to the settlement.
Conrad Weiser knew Shamokin well, frequenting the town as
diplomat and agent of the colonial government. Naturalist John
Bartram readily recognized the significance of the location
on his first visit and concluded "that we may reasonably hope,
when these parts shall be better known, that a beneficial trade"
would extend the reach of the English colonies to the Mississippi River.[4] Shamokin was home to such a complicated array

of humanity that historian James Merrell aptly described it as a "carnival of people and cultures."[5]

From this vantage point it is not hard to understand why Shamokin stands out in Hannah's memory. It is difficult to know with any certainty why her father left. It is impossible to know why he never returned. Hannah's father may have gone to Shamokin simply to join hunting parties to provide for his family. Another possibility is that he acted not as an individual but as a member of a kin-based group that honored obligations beyond the immediate needs of his family. As a member of the Brandywine Lenape, he may have gone to Shamokin to meet with members of Checochinican's followers or other Delawares who for some time made their homes along the Susquehanna River before moving further west. By midcentury Shamokin was the main point of communication and contact between Delawares who had settled in the western reaches of Pennsylvania and those who remained, in smaller and smaller enclaves, closer to their historic homelands. He may have responded to a call to witness trade or treaty negotiations that involved those to whom he owed allegiance. One of these explanations or any combination is worthy of consideration, but his failure to return remains a mystery. Shamokin was a violent town situated in a contact zone between competing Indian and colonial claims that seethed and roiled with a potential explosive power harboring catastrophic consequences not only for Hannah Freeman and her family but for all the Indian peoples living in Pennsylvania.

The disappearance of Hannah's father was not nearly as disastrous for her family as it might have been for an English, German, or Welsh family living in the same area. Colonial households were hierarchically organized, with the father the head. He was the spiritual and economic leader of the family unit and much depended upon his decisions and leadership. While everyone in a colonial Chester County family contributed to the daily life of this agricultural community, the death or abandonment of the male head of household almost always required another male relative to take his place in order for the family to continue living successfully. For Hannah's colonial counterparts, this loss most often meant remarriage if the wife was of an age to do so. In other circumstances, for instance, in the case of an elderly woman, a son or brother would take on the leadership role. In the worst scenarios, women and their children became dependent on the county's charity, ending up indentured and homeless. Whatever the circumstance of her father's departure, how Hannah's family experienced this loss varied greatly from her colonial neighbors. While Quakers were known for their more egalitarian approach to the roles men and women played in the Society of Friends, they organized their families and households similar to their non-Quaker colonial settlers.

Lenape families were not hierarchically structured but delineated across matrilineal lines.[6] Hannah's kin at the time of her father's departure included her maternal grandmother, Jane, her mother, Sarah, and her maternal aunts, Nanny and Betty. She also referenced another aunt without naming her and another grandmother who was part of this extended family. While this clearly establishes the centrality of a matrilineal organization in her collection of relatives, it is important to understand that Hannah's father was not the only male member. Hannah Freeman had two younger brothers who were born in the same cabin as she on William Webb's property. We don't know their names or what became of them. Of all her female kin, some surely had husbands, fathers, brothers, and sons who were part of this Brandywine community, but we have only a passing reference to an uncle or two. There is little doubt that warfare, disease, and the endemic violence prevalent in the colony took many Indian men away from their families during this period. However, the balanced, complementary organization of Lenape extended families aided their recovery of such personal loss. The subsistence of their community depended on their ability to plant corn and tend their gardens, work that was organized largely by women. Hannah clearly remembered that by the 1750s, the illegal parceling of the Brandywine Lenape lands guaranteed by treaty denied them access to some of their cornfields in Newlin, along the northern reaches of the river tract. In turn, colonial expansion caused their male kin to leave their families for longer periods of time in order to provide food. After her father's departure, the practical solution for Hannah's family was to move further south, where fewer restrictions made her family's use of the lands to plant gardens, gather resources, and harvest the bounty available along the river's floodplain much simpler.

Hannah and her extended family moved to "Centre in Christiana Hundred, New Castle County and lived in a cabin on Swithin Chandler's place."[7] Christiana Hundred was sandwiched between the southern reaches of the Brandywine River to the east and Red Clay Creek to the west. There was little difference between these lands and those lying further north, with the exception that the new home place put more space between her family and some of the major colonial thoroughfares that crisscrossed Chester County. Swithin Chandler was an heir to lands that were part of William Penn's first purchases. The Chandler family looms large in some of the more mythological history of Quaker relations with the Indians. According to local lore, Swithin Chandler's grandmother arrived in Philadelphia as a widow due to her husband dying during the transatlantic journey. With no money, no husband, and eight or nine children to care for, Widow Chandler moved into one of the caves that dotted the banks of the Delaware River, close to the city. Her future looked bleak, to say the least. As the story goes, passing Lenapes eventually took pity on her condition and began to bring her food and supplies, bridging the perilous gap until she found a second husband and a home for her children.[8] This local story was such an important part of region's iconography that it was used in a Philadelphia bank advertisement in 1919. The ad, headed "When ye Indians brought presents to the Chandler Children," warned readers of the importance of "laying by money for that possible day of disaster."[9] Despite the possible embellishments added to the various iterations of this tale, it does have some grounding in fact. The Swithin family, descended from Ann Swithin, claimed title to lands both on the Delaware side of the border and in Chester County. In Chester County those lands lying adjacent to the western banks of the Brandywine River were part of the Brandywine Lenapes' treaty claims. Perhaps Swithin Chandler and his extended family knew this all too well and acknowledged this reality by offering no resistance to the summer relocation of Hannah's home to his farm. Well beyond not interfering with this relocation, the Chandler family continued to play a large part in Hannah's life both as employers and as benefactors. This personal sense of obligation expressed by the Chandlers and other families living on Hannah's homelands spanned generations and cannot be lightly dismissed.

While Hannah and her family did settle in cabins across the Delaware border, they continued to travel back and forth between the Swithin Chandler farm and Kennett Township in Chester County, where Hannah and her brothers were born. The connections between Kennett Township and Christiana Hundred are fairly easy to see. Geographically they are contiguous parcels divided only by a colonial boundary that was disputed for decades by the proprietors of Maryland and Pennsylvania. A royal commission ordered a survey of the boundary in 1760 to resolve this dispute. Today we know this boundary as the Mason-Dixon line. Surprisingly, some portion of the physical boundary between the two colonies remained in dispute as late as the 1920s. The allegiance of the Quaker immigrants who settled these parcels lay largely with Pennsylvania's Quaker-led government and not Maryland's assembly. A quick study of land parcels in the mid-eighteenth century shows that the Chandlers, Harlans, Baldwins, and Mendenhalls owned parcels that transected the colonial boundaries and also fell within the Brandywine Lenape treaty lands.[10] These Quaker families were connected by more than property boundaries: they were related by blood and marriage, shared first names as well as last names, and belonged to more than one Quaker congregation at a time. The membership rolls of the Quaker meetings in Kennett and Christiana Hundred clearly demonstrate the interconnectedness of these families—as well as pose a challenge to a historian's detective skills. The Harlan family gave land for the building of the Kennett Monthly Meeting and also hosted the Centre Monthly Meetings in their home. Both congregations met variously at Kennett and Centre as weather and other circumstances determined.[11] The names are a who's who compendium of families that not only intersected Hannah Freeman's life but are also the same names intimately connected to the Brandywine Lenapes' dispossession. From her birth to her death, the Brintons, Chandlers, Harlans, Marshalls, Pierces, Taylors, and Webbs were a part of Hannah Freeman's destiny.

Hannah Freeman's move to Kennett and Centre also signaled change for her Quaker neighbors and sheds light on how they understood their relationship to her as a member of the Brandywine Lenapes and also how Quakers began to reconsider their larger political and social responsibilities. Quaker prosperity and leadership between the time of Penn's death and the outbreak of the French and Indian War led to ideological shifts in their religious convictions. Many prosperous Quakers in southeastern Pennsylvania turned their attention away from the cultivation of their "inner plantations" in favor of building their "outer plantations."[12] This philosophical shift to promoting material prosperity and the accumulation of political power and wealth, rather than focusing on the health and well-being of their inner light, caused Quakers to place little priority on their neighborly relationship with the Delawares. Instead they emphasized economic stability and secured alliances with Indian tribes that stood to offer the greatest advantages in trade and territorial expansion. The provincial government of Pennsylvania, dominated by Quakers, perceived the Delawares as an obstacle to securing land for the colony, while they considered the Iroquois as more politically and economically strategic friends. The provincial government's main concern regarding the Delawares living east of the Appalachian Mountains was to dispossess them of their lands and place them under the hegemony of the Iroquois Confederacy. Delawares resisted these political maneuvers on most fronts, often reminding Quakers of Penn's promise in their appeals to the provincial government. The Quaker-controlled assembly held Penn's vision in high esteem and invoked it when advantageous, but the practicalities of running a successful colony and reaping the temporal benefits allowed the Quakers to abandon many of their humanitarian goals in favor of newer material objectives and greater political power.

One of the most devastating demonstrations of this new shift in Quaker political strategies was the Walking Purchase of 1737.[13] This singular episode in Pennsylvania's colonial history served as a pivot point between those who defended the altruistic and benevolent aims of William Penn's Indian policies and those who flaunted the treaty as irreproachable evidence of the proprietors' legacy of fraud. At the heart of the controversy was an earlier deed purportedly signed by William Penn and Lenape leaders granting Penn land between the forks of the Delaware as "much as could be covered in a days walk." James Logan hired three runners to cover a much greater expanse of land than the Lenapes were prepared to cede. Armed with suspect documents and a threadbare attachment to William Penn's promise to deal fairly with Pennsylvania's Indians, James Logan and Penn's sons duped the Lenapes into accepting terms that ultimately dispossessed them of one of their final contiguous holdings along the Delaware River in the Lehigh Valley. Even though the superintendent of Indian Affairs, William Johnson, exonerated the colony's proprietors in 1762, scholars continue to challenge the legitimacy of the purchase.[14] Most recently Andrew Newman cited the episode as a "case study for the colonial abuse of literacy, because the proprietors both insisted on and exploited the letter of the agreement, abrogating the spirit of land transactions established by the Pennsylvania founder and his native counterparts."[15] The fraudulent Walking Purchase permanently tarnished the Quakers' reputation among the Delawares. In the years after Penn's death in 1718, the historic alliance between the Lenapes and Quakers came under great strain, but the fraudulent Walking Purchase of 1737 continues to be remembered by many modern Delawares as the singular event that led to the loss of their ancestral homelands in Pennsylvania. As recently as 2004 the Delaware Nation, one of three federally recognized nations of Delawares in the United States, filed suit in the District Court for the Eastern District of Pennsylvania seeking the restoration of 314 acres originally parceled in the Walking Purchase. The court dismissed the case. The Delaware Nation appealed to the Third Circuit Court two years later, but the original dismissal was upheld. In one final tenacious attempt to rectify what modern Delawares still consider an outright betrayal, they submitted the case to the Supreme Court, which refused the case based on a need for further review by the lower courts.[16]

Ideological shifts are difficult to measure, but as James Logan and William Penn's heirs envisioned a bountiful treasury and expansive boundaries for their colony, Chester County's Quaker constituents expressed the changing ideology in their enthusiasm for profiteering. Nathaniel Newlin suffered no qualms of conscience when he illegally parceled and sold the Brandywine Lenapes' treaty lands, nor did he show any hesitance in making a profit, even though his own government ordered that he stop his activities. Another example of local Quakers' disregard for the health of their "inner plantations" was the series of "dam wars" recounted in the provincial assembly records, as Chester County farmers competed to control and limit the Brandywine River's flow to serve their privately owned grist mills. As quickly as one farmer built a new gristmill along the river, another filed a complaint against his neighbor further upstream for ruining his business. The assembly ordered some of these dams removed, but found few permanent solutions for these disputes. As the assembly negotiated settlers' litigation, it gave little regard to the Lenapes' regularly recorded claims that their families were starving because the mills prohibited access to the vital fish supply.

In 1743 the Philadelphia Yearly Meeting, the central governing body of the Society of Friends, authored and distributed a list of twelve questions to be read at the monthly meetings, including those at Centre and Kennett.[17] This administrative action further signaled the growing concerns of Quaker leaders for the spiritual well-being of their extremely successful constituents. The questions asked their members to reflect on their actions and to consider whether or not they were *living* their faith, one of the basic tenets of their religion. Reform-minded Quakers were disturbed at the growing trend among their prosperous members to ignore or abandon their responsibility to teach and represent "the Truth." Foremost among the trends that troubled elder Quakers was the quest, accumulation, and display of material wealth. John Woolman, a Quaker preacher most well known for his antislavery stance, reminded his fellow Friends, "Ye cannot serve God and mammon."[18] This was not an easy message to deliver to an audience reaping the rewards of colonial land acquisition and the blossoming colonial economy. Quakers living in Chester County were some of the wealthiest members of their society. Hannah Freeman's presence and the visibility of the many Indian peoples who worked in Quaker homes and fields must have served as a daily reminder of a troubling reality. Their new wealth and prosperity was built upon the loss and dispossession of their former Lenape friends. As certainly as the brutal Spanish conquest of Mexico's indigenous populations fueled the wealth and expansion of the Spanish empire, the pacifist Quakers were largely responsible for a benevolent conquest that produced similar results. By midcentury this Quaker call to consciousness led to permanent change

Lenapehoking Lost

in the Society's membership in many ways, but one of the most profound changes was the role that the Quaker community played in Indian affairs. On the local level this ideological shift may explain why Hannah Freeman, her family, and other Delaware families met little resistance as they moved freely across their ancient homelands and why they found acceptance and support from their Quaker neighbors. Perhaps the Quakers' silence signaled their acknowledgment of this past wrong. Perhaps the generosity they extended Hannah Freeman and her kin was their attempt to "tend their inner plantations."

The incongruous coupling of hunger for prosperity and power with a doctrine of pacifism was an ideological train wreck for Quakers in colonial Pennsylvania. Eventually the Society's members found their way back to the fundamental tenets of their faith, but only after their political agenda had completely alienated the Delawares living in Pennsylvania, turning their former allies and friends into enemies. The Quaker dissolution of their "ancient friendship" with the Delawares had many beginnings, including the orchestration of the fraudulent Walking Purchase in 1737. Not only did the Walking Purchase finally dismantle the eastern Delawares' stronghold, it formally recognized Iroquois land claims and political authority over the Lenapes in Pennsylvania. The relationship between the colony and the Iroquois was long in the making. William Penn and his heirs and successors believed the Iroquois Confederacy was perhaps the most important link in their diplomatic strategy with Native Americans in their colony. Not long after taking control of the colony, Penn realized that the various Lenape communities, with their dispersed settlement patterns, were unable to offer adequate access to the fur trade or even the unified political voice that colonial authorities most coveted. The desire to tap into the lucrative fur trade is easy to understand, but the complicated, often overlapping, Lenape land-ownership patterns proved less than efficient for colonial authorities who sought a quick, peaceful path to land acquisition and Lenape dispossession.

The Iroquois not only offered a more unified and manageable front for diplomatic relations, their leadership also suggested that they had the power to control Lenape diplomacy and dominate any political affairs in which the Lenape sachems claimed to voice authority. This contest of power between the Lenapes and the Iroquois is an old story, told in greater depth by other scholars. But suffice it to say that by the 1740s the Iroquois Confederacy dominated diplomatic relations with the Pennsylvania government, and the Lenapes both east and west of the mountains seemed to be little more than a local management issue for the provincial government and its Indian agents. Together the Pennsylvania government and the Iroquois Confederacy created a bitter legacy that Delawares on both sides of the Appalachian Mountains would not forget. William Penn's vision of a peaceable kingdom was nowhere to be found when James Logan looked forward to the day when no Delawares lived in Pennsylvania, especially those "vile ones from the Forks of the Delaware River."[19]

The Delawares who moved into western Pennsylvania were not alone in their growing anger and disaffection toward their former English neighbors, nor had they severed their ties with kin who remained in the east. Along with other Indian refugees who increasingly sought homelands separate from colonial settlements, Delawares found community and kinship with new allies, even including a number of Iroquois who were also disenchanted with the political machinations of their own nations. Delawares, Senecas, and Shawnees created new homes in western Pennsylvania, believing that physical and political boundaries would allow them to live in relative peace in their new homelands. But again, this was not to be. Western Pennsylvania was the site of an increasingly contentious border between the French and British empires in North America. Throughout the eighteenth century England, France, and Spain challenged and rechallenged their respective North American boundaries: Queen Anne's War (1702–13), the War of Jenkins' Ear (1739–

Lenapehoking Lost

48), and King George's War (1740–48). Each time treaties were made, boundaries were drawn, but little was settled. Each colonial war largely disregarded the Indian inhabitants of the lands. Expansion was the ultimate objective of the European interests and consequently no settlement lasted long. King George's War, known as the War of Austrian Succession, was a colonial war fought throughout Europe, with North America being a distant but important theater of the war. The war ended with the Treaty of Aix-la-Chapelle, an uneasy agreement at best. A peace was concluded that satisfied no one—not the French or British Crowns, not their colonial representatives in North America, and especially not the land-hungry settlers who were already moving across the Appalachian Mountains into western lands.

The Indian communities settled in western Pennsylvania in 1748 were unaware that a treaty signed in a distant land would eventually embroil all of them in what some consider the first "world war." The French and English agreed to an uncertain boundary that both sides had every intention of contesting. Neither side had definitive information on the exact physical location of the boundary line because only the Indians who lived there and a few colonial traders knew the territory intimately. The English and French were not alone in the uncertainty of their claims. Pennsylvania and Virginia colonies made independent declarations that extended their colonial borders to an uncertain and unknowable western boundary. Unfortunately, colonial boundaries, imperial declarations, and royal pretensions are only a small part of empire building. In the end perhaps the most important aspect of colonization is occupation, and the French made the first play to establish their occupation of the disputed boundary. By 1749 Captain Celeron de Bienville, with great ceremony, ventured to show French occupation. Journeying from Montreal to the Ohio River, at each stop he displayed the French coat of arms and planted a lead plate that declared French ownership of all the lands guaranteed in the treaty. With each "Vive le roi!" Celeron defied challengers to unseat the French claims from the Great Lakes to the Ohio River valley and the Mississippi River. He set in motion events that would reach deep into Indian settlements.

Hannah Freeman did not know about Celeron's trip and she did not know the diplomatic and military maneuverings that would soon initiate a war between the French, English, and the various Indian communities. But what Hannah Freeman did know is that violence altered her way of life. Distant Delaware kin initiated and implemented acts of violence against settlers closer and closer to the Brandywine valley. At the same time Pennsylvania settlers' growing indiscriminate hatred of all Indians fueled vigilante actions throughout the colony. Hannah Freeman and her family may have chosen to remain on their ancestral homelands in southeastern Pennsylvania while the center of the Lenapes' world moved further and further west. But that distance did not necessarily signal a complete and permanent break in communication or their relationships with their people, no matter where they lived. Hannah and her family continued to make their living from a land that was crisscrossed with ancient Indian roads and pathways that led to Philadelphia, the diplomatic center of the colony. Indian messengers and visitors made regular visits from the western lands to the colonial capital, bringing news and diplomatic instructions. It is hard to imagine that Delawares living in the west did not stop and talk with relatives, friends, and sachems in route to the City of Brotherly Love. Despite the extensive settlement of colonists throughout southeastern Pennsylvania, this old landscape probably still held sacred sites and places of ceremony the western Lenapes were compelled to visit. It is even probable that occasionally they found shelter with relatives and friends like Hannah and her kin.

However Hannah Freeman and her family came to know the larger political and military drama that was looming, the news of violence struck closer and closer to home. The French and Indian War began in Pennsylvania when a young George Washington, acting as the leader of a small Virginia regiment, challenged the authority of the French empire at Fort Duquesne, the site of modern-day Pittsburgh. Washington's diplomatic declaration of English claims in 1754 was met with a restrained response on the part of fort's French commander. Washington retreated from Fort Duquesne but defiantly built a rude and rough fort in a small valley some fifty miles southeast, where he prepared to take a stand for English empire. In the end the French and their numerous Indian allies forced Washington to surrender his hastily constructed Fort Necessity. Although many consider this military confrontation one of the opening salvos of the war, it was not until the following year, 1755, that both the British and French monarchs launched campaigns to protect and preserve their respective boundary claims from Nova Scotia to the Ohio River. Delawares living east and west of the Appalachians had generations of experience that caused them to distrust the British when the French and Indian War began. General Braddock, commander of one of the British expeditions against the French in western Pennsylvania, arrogantly proclaimed, "No savage should inherit the land."[20] English arrogance, coupled with the demands of their closest and oldest allies, eventually caused western Delawares to take a stand in this global war. Rather than attacking the British along the disputed boundaries in the west, the Delawares took their part of the war back to their ancient homelands, striking settlements across the Delaware River in New Jersey. In 1755 the backcountry of Pennsylvania exploded in a series of attacks that historian Jane Merritt convincingly argues were personal and intimate.[21] Delawares, with Shawnee allies, attacked individual families, trade outposts, and missionary settlements. They left signs on both property and bodies proclaiming that the English, who were formerly their friends and neighbors, were now enemies. Between 1755 and 1757 Delawares attacked, killed, and scalped men, women, and children living between the Delaware and Susquehanna rivers. These killings, according to Merritt, were personal, often directed at those among whom the Delawares had worked, traded, and prayed. On one hand they targeted specific settler communities with which they had long-standing disputes. In particular those who settled in the lands lost through the Walking Treaty were driven from their homes. Other times warring Delawares warned particular families who were perceived as undeserving of this revenge to abandon their homes before the violence began. Even eastern Delawares, who had converted to Christianity and were living among Moravian missions, were not spared. The backcountry of eastern Pennsylvania was in chaos, leaving no one trusting anyone: not Quakers, not settlers, and especially not the Indians who still lived there. John Bartram expressed the fear and anger caused by these personal attacks: Indians who now obliterated "all before them with fire ball and tomahawk" were the same ones whom he remembered as "intimate playmates."[22] The Delawares who went to war against Pennsylvania were unleashing a fury that that had been generations in the making. Perhaps it was the remembrance of Penn's failed promise that intensified their bitterness and caused their explosive actions. In the mid-eighteenth century the Delawares living east and west of the Appalachian Mountains understood that all English were unwilling to honor treaties or share land. To this ideology there were no exceptions.

Hannah Freeman's family and other Lenapes living in the war zone responded in diverse ways to this renewed era of violence. Some were encouraged to join their western kin and Shawnee war parties, and many did. Others moved closer to colonial settlements where they were known and understood to be noncombatants. We do not know if Hannah's brothers or her uncles joined the fighting or chose not to pick up arms, but we do know that the news of the atrocities and anxiety emanating from this war zone did have an impact on Hannah Freeman, her family, and her Quaker neighbors. The eight assemblymen representing Chester County in the provincial government were finding it more and more impossible to refuse the demands of Pennsylvania's citizens to provide monies for the support of a militia. Not only was England engaged in a war against France, but that war was disrupting trade and creating havoc throughout the colony. Non-Quaker members of the assembly and their constituents increasingly accused the Quakers of doing more to protect the Indians in the colony than they did to provide defense for the settlers who lived miles from Philadelphia. There was some truth in that. At midcentury the majority of the eight men representing Chester County in the provincial assembly were members of Quaker families who knew Hannah Freeman. Thomas Chandler's, Joseph Gibbons's, and Nathaniel Pennock's families all provided care for Hannah Freeman later in her life.[23] In 1755 two of Chester County's Quaker assemblymen resigned their seats "because many of our Constituents seem of the Opinion that our present Situation of Public Affairs call upon us for services in a military Way, which, from a conviction of Judgment . . . we cannot comply with," and the following year, after Pennock and Peter Dicks, another Quaker legislator, were reelected "without solicitation," both promptly resigned their seats at the opening session in October 1756 as a protest against the colony's militarization.[24]

As Quaker assemblymen took an ethical stand against war, they also hurled accusations at the settlers at the front line of the violence, many of them Scots-Irish Presbyterians who did not hold legal title to their properties. Illegal squatters were a critical variable in Pennsylvania's expansion throughout the eighteenth century. The proprietors encouraged, ignored, or reprimanded those settlers who fenced and built homes on lands to which they had no legal title, depending on where and when the settlements took place. In the earlier decades of Pennsylvania's history, those illegal squatters who parceled lands guaranteed by treaty were occasionally reprimanded but rarely evicted from the lands. They provided an essential component of Pennsylvania's benevolent Indian policy, forcing a simple but determined dispossession by parceling, fencing, and making other "improvements" on Indian properties. This is especially evident in the case of Hannah's sachem, Checochinican, and the Brandywine Lenape. As the colony became more settled and Pennsylvania's diplomatic strategies changed, the illegal squatters in the western and northern outreaches of the colony threatened to undermine treaties made with the Iroquois, who exerted authority over much of unsettled Pennsylvania. These extralegal land practices were a threat to the colony's security and productivity. The proprietors, concerned with offending their Iroquois allies, ordered the eviction of illegal squatters and went so far as to send expeditions in 1748, 1750, and 1768 to rout these settlements, to the point of burning houses and barns and arresting the squatters. Governor Thomas Penn despised the backcountry squatters as the "lower sort of people . . . who are ungovernable." His provincial secretary, Richard Peters, oversaw many of these evictions, observing that "the worst sort of Irish" were regular offenders of the colony's land laws.[25]

For Hannah Freeman and other noncombatant Indians living in eastern Pennsylvania, the immediate threat was clear. The majority of colonial Pennsylvanians perceived no difference between friendly, neutral, or enemy Indian communities. In 1756 Governor Robert Morris legitimized this sentiment by declaring war against the Delawares. To further this cause the colony offered a bounty on "enemy" Delaware scalps: 130 Spanish dollars for male Indians over twelve years of age and 50 Spanish dollars for Indian women.[26] It takes little imagination to understand how Pennsylvania's armed response put every Indian life in jeopardy. All the Quaker benevolence in the world had little chance of resisting the virulent Indian-hating sentiment that permeated William Penn's peaceable kingdom in 1756. Even though Hannah's closest neighbors were stalwart in their nonviolent conviction, they were unable to prevent the violence that gripped the colony. Like many other Indian families in southeastern Pennsylvania, Hannah's found safety by moving closer to more densely populated colonial settlements. In 1758 Han-

Lenapehoking Lost

nah left her home on the Brandywine River and moved closer to Philadelphia. There she joined some of her relatives who made their home along Chester Creek only fifteen miles from the colonial capital and ten miles from the Delaware River and the border between Pennsylvania and New Jersey. For over a year Hannah remained with her aunts Nanny and Betty and their husbands and children. During this time she continued to make her living working for local farmers: spinning, sewing, basket making, and taking advantage of other domestic opportunities. Her closest Quaker neighbor on Chester Creek was Joseph Chamberlin who, like his Quaker neighbors closer to the Brandywine River, registered no official objections to the Lenape cabins on his property. He was a member of a prominent Quaker family and the Concord Meeting.

Pennsylvania's war against the Delawares was not a sustained one. Quakers working outside official avenues of the provincial assembly initiated talks that brought the warring sides together to discuss terms of peace. Israel Pemberton, one of the founders of the Friendly Association for Regaining and Preserving Peace with the Indians by Pacific Measures (later shortened to the Friendly Association), opened his home to representatives of the Iroquois and western Delawares to explore their complaints against the colonial government. Scaroudy, speaking for the western tribes, commended the Quakers' pacifist intentions yet shrewdly noted that "it was now so long since we had heard anything about them [the Quakers], we had concluded that when brother Onas [William Penn] dyed that Spirit dyed with him."[27] Indeed, Quaker peacemakers revived William Penn's peace testimony and found a renewed political life as Indian agents and diplomats. Quaker commitment to Native American communities continues to the present day. Subsequently, the Treaty of Easton, signed late in 1758, effectively stilled the open hostilities between the western Delawares and colonial Pennsylvanians and also assured the provincial government that the Delawares would not enter the war fighting for the French. But the peace was uneasy at best. Most colonial settlers in Pennsylvania perceived all Indians as "savages"; there were few who believed that Indians and settlers could coexist as neighbors.

The following spring Hannah Freeman returned to her homestead on William Webb's property along the Brandywine River.[28] Awaiting her was the familiar routine of working for Quaker neighbors, sometimes sewing, sometimes churning, and sometimes healing the sick. Hannah planted her garden, tended her pigs and cows, and occasionally rode her horse throughout the neighborhood. News of the war traveled the paths that ran the breadth and length of Chester County, but the seasonal routine of this agricultural community remained steady and little changed. For southeastern Pennsylvanians the war was fought at enough distance that there was little disruption to their daily lives. Chester County was especially buffered from the war because the residents were insulated by the prevalence of the Quaker community. In 1760 the region remained a fairly homogenous population of tax-paying, Quaker, English subjects who owned some of the most valuable land in British North America. For those interested in pursuing an avocation as diplomats for Indian affairs, it was a safe, stable home base. For Indian families who wanted nothing more than to live peacefully on their homelands, Chester County was their best, even if not their safest, prospect in Pennsylvania.

Despite the best efforts of Quaker and Indian diplomats to negotiate terms that kept open warfare at bay, racialized tensions seethed just beneath the surface. The 1758 treaty proved to be little more than a brief interval in the violence before new hostilities broke out between frontier settlers and Indian war parties. Reports of atrocities and rumors of unified Indian attacks percolated throughout Pennsylvania, sometimes true and other times not.

Most Indians living in the western reaches of the colony understood English objectives all too well. No matter what efforts were made to control the rapid settlement of their colony's western boundary, the rapacious hunger of land speculators and squatters willing to defy the law made clear to Native American leadership that the English objective was land, land, and more land. Indian allies understood that the only thing that preserved that boundary was a highly militarized border recognized by both factions. The success of such a line required a level of Indian unity among the various factions unlike any known in recent history. Part of the inspiration for this new pan-Indian collaboration emanated from a series of prophetic visions and messages spreading through Indian country in the mid-eighteenth century. One of the most well-known and influential prophets who offered such a message was a Delaware man known as Neolin. Neolin's birthplace is unknown, but his message first gained traction in the Ohio country. His message echoed earlier prophecies first heard on the Susquehanna River a decade earlier. Neolin communicated through vision and prayer with the Master of Life and advocated what historian Gregory Dowd described as a separation theology.[29] Neolin believed that the cause of the suffering of all Indian peoples lay in their association with "white people." He urged a gradual separation from involvement with European material culture and society in general, and he also advocated a new spiritual foundation for the amalgamated Indian communities then settled in western Pennsylvania and Ohio. Neolin offered a new beginning for Delawares, Shawnees, and countless other peoples who anxiously searched for solutions to their "colonial problem." Fundamental to that solution was the permanent separation of Indian peoples and English subjects. The news of the prophets undoubtedly reached the communities of Indians living behind the colonial frontiers as well as beyond it. How did Hannah and her kin respond to these messages of separatism that so strongly warned of the dangers of close association with colonial settlements? Did the news of visions, dreams, and prophecies further fracture their families and towns? Hannah and so many Native Americans living deep within colonial set-

7. John Wilmer, *Massacre of Indians at Lancaster by Paxton Boys*, 1841.
(Courtesy of the American Philosophical Society,
Philadelphia)

tlement throughout the Atlantic seaboard faced similar challenges to their own beliefs. All made the decision to survive.
But their strategies were all encompassing.

Not surprisingly, English diplomats and strategists came to
similar conclusions. War was a costly business and no matter
what colonial legislation and control was exerted on the settler
populations, wherever Indian borders met backcountry settlements violence was the order of the day. Colonial agents could
do little to control the hemorrhaging frontier. As the French
and Indian War drew to an end in North America, British strategists determined that the best solution was to delineate a clear
and separate boundary between Indian land and the colonial
settlements. The Royal Proclamation of 1763 essentially drew a
line that that shadowed the Appalachian Mountains as it passed
through Pennsylvania. While this seemed like a reasonable beginning to prevent further warfare, the British quickly established a series of outposts that were supposed to make this line
on a map a real and respected border. However, before the ink

Lenapehoking Lost

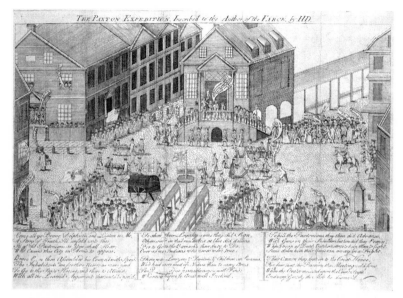

8. Henry Dawkins, *Preparations in Philadelphia to Prepare for the Arrival of the Paxton Boys*, 1764. (Courtesy of the American Philosophical Society, Philadelphia)

was dry on the proclamation, Pennsylvania squatters, in total defiance of the boundary, moved into western Pennsylvania, enraging the Indian peoples living there. Once more the colony was enmeshed in bloodshed.

The Native American response to the renewed hostilities took a new form, this time in a series of aggressions that are collectively known as Pontiac's Rebellion. In the spring of 1763 unified Native American warriors attacked thirteen British outposts situated in these western territories. Five of these forts were positioned approximate to the Proclamation Line as it ran through Pennsylvania: Fort Presque Isle, Fort Le Beouf, Fort Venango, Fort Pitt, and Fort Ligonier. Only Forts Pitt and Ligonier withstood the assaults; unified Indian forces in which the Delawares were strongly represented took the other three forts. The motivations for the attacks were as diverse as the Native American communities represented, but the repeated failure of British authorities to control illegal settlement of lands coupled with the prophetic message delivered by Neolin and others created a heady brew for Indian peoples who were weary and frustrated with English politics. The hostilities escalated through the spring of 1764, with Delaware attacks making their way, once again, to the Susquehanna River valley. Eventually British forces would prevail, and a series of treaties negotiated yet another uneasy peace between the Indian factions and the British.[30] But settlers living in the Susquehanna valley and the hinterlands of Pennsylvania's colonial settlement were not appeased—in fact, their frustration with the provincial government and their hatred of all Indians reached all the way to Hannah Freeman's cabin on the Brandywine River.

On December 14, 1763, as skirmishes raged in the western parts of the colony, a loosely organized group of vigilantes burned Conestoga Town, only half a day's walk from the Brandywine River, to the ground. The largely Christian Conestoga community had a relationship with the proprietary government reaching back to 1701. This community, not unlike the small enclaves along the Brandywine River and Chester Creek was made up of approximately twenty men, women, and children who made their living like Hannah Freeman and her family. They had gardens, bartered and sold baskets and brooms, and most likely found occasional labor with local farmers. Their neighbors knew them by their English names: George, Bill, Peggy, Sally, and Jacob, to name a few. They dressed for the most part in English clothing and lived in cabins like their colonial neighbors. They were known throughout the region as peaceful neighbors. But on that December morning the colonial hatred, anxiety, and frustration proved to be lethal. When the vigilantes descended on the community, they found only six residents at home. All were brutally murdered and scalped. The other fourteen members of this kin-based community were at a local iron works selling their baskets and brooms. The survivors, under the charge of the local sheriff, were gathered in the Lancaster blockhouse for their own protection. But thirteen days later, in

Lenapehoking Lost

a fury of hatred, the "Paxton Boys," a loose band of Scots-Irish settlers, rode into Lancaster and killed the rest of the Conestoga community. The murders were brutal, and no one was spared from mutilation. Men, women, and children as young as three years old were scalped, their hands amputated by a group of men who had no personal grievance against any member of this community. For the Paxton Boys the Conestogas were guilty of one crime—being Indian—and it was enough. The sheriff and members of the Lancaster community, who had ultimately failed to protect the Conestogas, later protested to the outraged governor, claiming they had tried to prevent the massacre. Brutal as this attack was, it was not exceptional—in fact, it mirrored the kind of violence that was endemic to the Pennsylvania frontier in this era. But this particular episode escalated into a seething backcountry rebellion aimed at the provincial government in Philadelphia.

After the massacre the Paxton Boys took their grievances to Philadelphia, armed with the same black-and-white logic they had used to rationalize the executions of unarmed innocents. They saw the provincial government, run by elite Anglicans and Quakers, as a threat to their own survival. In February 1764 over 250 militiamen marched on Philadelphia with the intent of killing another group of peaceful Indians then being held for their own protection in the city's barracks. Fortunately, a volunteer regiment, led by Benjamin Franklin, met the militiamen just outside the city and defused the rebellion through negotiations. In the aftermath of the rebellion, both sides hurled accusations at the other. Ben Franklin called the men who had committed the atrocities "Christian White savages," while the vigilantes shot back "that men in Power refuse to relieve their sufferings" on the frontier.[31] Little was resolved in this confrontation between the provincial government and its distant backcountry constituents. But for those Indian peoples living in Pennsylvania behind the frontier line and for Hannah Freeman, there was no safety in Pennsylvania: not in Philadelphia, not in Chester County. The largely Scots-Irish members of this vigilante group murdered the Conestoga Indians because they believed there were no "friendly" Indians, only enemies.

In 1764 Hannah Freeman, "being afraid" because of the Conestoga murders, "moved over the Delaware to New Jersey and lived with the Jersey Indians."[32] For the first time in her life, Hannah Freeman left her beloved Brandywine River home for an extended length of time. We do not know if she went at the urging of her neighbors or whether she and members of her community made this decision independently from their Quaker friends. What a hardship it must have been for her to leave her small farm, her gardens, and her household. We do not know if she left suddenly as the "Paxton Boys" marched through the area or if she had some time to prepare for her trip. However, as Hannah's exile began, the political events that embroiled the colony from Philadelphia to the Ohio River extended ripples of violence, fear, and anxiety that finally touched Hannah Freeman in an undeniably personal way. How this exile would change her life was hard to see as she made her way across the broad span of the Delaware River. Did she worry that she might not ever see her home again? Was she now, like countless numbers of Lenapes before her, torn loose from her homeland, exiled indefinitely? One thing was obviously clear to Hannah Freeman and her kin as they made their exodus to New Jersey: not even their Quaker neighbors, armed with benevolent intentions, political authority, and economic clout could protect her family from the vengeance of the backcountry settlers.

CHAPTER FIVE

Kindness Extended

The Lenape people had many stories handed down from generation to generation that told of their history and culture. Elders told stories of the creator, Kishelemukong, who caused a giant turtle to rise from the depths of the ocean to become the land upon which all beings lived: Turtle Island. First Man and First Woman sprouted from a tree that grew on the turtle's back.[1] They learned to live in a world populated with seen and unseen forces, dealt with loss, faced danger, and enjoyed abundance. As a young girl Hannah probably heard these stories, which merged the Lenapes' identity as a people with the lands they called home. Not only did the stories teach each new generation about the past, they also instructed Lenapes on how to live their lives everyday. Through these stories Hannah Freeman probably learned about the hardships her people had endured along the way. According to their ancient history, Hannah's people crossed lands fraught with danger and peril, sometimes starving and sometimes at war with other peoples, who challenged their right to pass. The story is one of sacrifice and endurance, change and resilience.[2] Before the ancient Lenape found their new homeland, they lost family and kin through separation and death, but they would find new alliances and form new kinships that increased their numbers and strengthened their culture. It is a story of long ago, yesterday, and today.

In 1763 Hannah crossed the Delaware River into New Jersey because her safety, like that of all Indians in Pennsylvania, was threatened. Did Hannah look back across the river that day and wonder if she would ever return to her home on the Brandy-wine River? Did she think about the stories told by her elders of the strength of her ancestors and their determination to find a good place to live? What a trial this journey must have been for Hannah and her family. However, knowing her people's history and the oral traditions passed down from generation to generation, she probably drew on the strength and resolve of her ancestors under adversity. Hannah was a Lenape woman, and the wisdom and power of all her grandmothers served her well during this time of hardship.

There is little evidence that tells us precisely what Hannah did during her seven years of exile from her home, but there are some indications that her Quaker friends on both sides of the Delaware River encouraged and supported her departure. New Jersey was not unlike Pennsylvania in the hysteria that gripped the colonial settlements as war raged in the backcountry. Rumors of enemy Indians "skulking" through their communities spread fear and anxiety throughout the region at regular intervals. New Jersey's citizens demanded protection from their own provincial government, calling for a militarized response. On some occasions, as was the case with the Conestoga Indians, local governments would lock their Indian neighbors in the local jail to prevent them from "committing any Outrages upon the People" and also for their own protection.[3] The fears of New Jersey's settler population were not unfounded. The same Delawares who led the attacks along Pennsylvania's frontier borders found allies across the Delaware River who had their own grievances to exercise. Consequently, settlers in the northern and southern reaches of the New Jersey colony, whether neighbor or enemy, perceived all Indians as a threat. Random attacks on settler farms, especially in the northern part of the colony, confirmed their worst fears.

Unprovoked crimes against innocent Indian families and the threat of losing legal control of the colony's frantic citizens spurred the governor to enact legislation that he hoped would

Kindness Extended

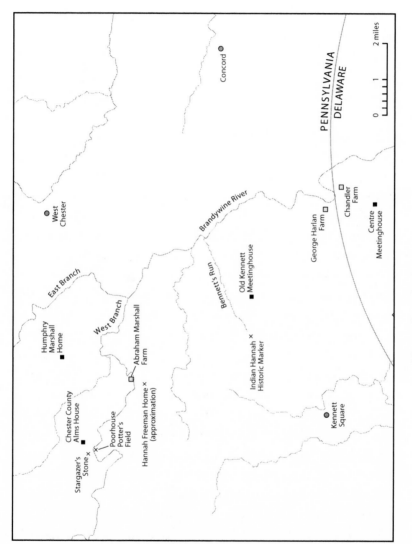

Map 4. Brandywine River valley.

prevent further unchecked violence. Governor Jonathan Belcher ordered the mustering of a militia, which found many enthusiastic participants, and ordered, with the assembly's support, the building of a series of blockhouses for the defense of this small colony. Northern New Jersey and its border with New York were most vulnerable and became the focus of the militarized activities. However, the governor also understood that there were enclaves and communities of Indian peoples living throughout New Jersey who sought protection from the anger and threat of their colonial neighbors. While colonists built blockhouses and organized militias throughout the colony, violent crimes against Indian peoples increased. Governor Belcher took a unique and unprecedented approach to solving his immediate problem, doing what he believed was in the best interest of noncombatant Indians living in the colony. In a proclamation issued December 3, 1755, the governor ordered all "Indians as are Really Friends" to appear before their county magistrate and register their "Fidelity to his Majesty and Attachment to their Brethren the English." The magistrate was to record their names, the names of their family members, and "natural descriptions as fully and Particularly as [he] can." Upon being registered, Indian men and women swore an oath of loyalty and were presented with a certificate, which were required to carry at all times. Further, to avoid any unfortunate "accident" of violence, the "loyal" Indians were also required to wear a red ribbon around their heads as visible proof just in case they found themselves "in any place where such an Accident may be likely to happen." To further secure the citizens of his colony, Governor Belcher ordered that any Indian man, woman, or child found without the ribbon and registration papers "shall be taken up and Carried before" the local magistrate. Without papers, Indians were confined in jail until they proved their loyalty or someone came forward to vouch for them.[4]

While New Jersey's settlers were not exceptionally empathetic to the plight of noncombatant Indians, the government did

Kindness Extended

prove to be much more effective in maintaining law and order throughout the colony, unlike Pennsylvania at this time. Settlers who committed unwarranted attacks on Indian peoples in the colony faced the full measure of the law. In the summer of 1756, settlers viciously attacked a family of Lenapes living in Somerset County, planning to sell their scalps for bounty in Philadelphia. The family consisted of father, mother, and three young children, all registered with the county as "friend Indians." In the middle of the night four men entered the cabin, attacking first the father who, though wounded, escaped to his neighbor's to raise the alarm. The four men then turned their wrath on the mother, who subsequently died from ax wounds to her head and body. The children, an eleven-year-old and infant twins, miraculously survived the attack due to the skillful administrations of the local doctor. The brutality displayed in this crime resembled the actions of the Paxton Boys in Pennsylvania. However, the local authorities acted swiftly to condemn the "villainous scheme" and seek justice for the family. Within a few short weeks, local authorities had captured all four men and placed them in the local jail. But despite the official stance condemning this violent crime, many New Jersey settlers in the region were sympathetic to the criminals. Before long, rumors of a planned jailbreak raised such concern that the governor ordered a regiment of the colony's militia posted outside the jail, twenty-four hours a day, until the criminals were brought to trial. The assigned regiment's purpose was not only to guard the jail to prevent escape, but also to protect the "Judges and Justices" conducting the investigation and trial until "the Court shall think it consistent with the Publick Safety that they may be discharged." Governor Belcher made his orders explicit: "The Officers & Soldiers are hereby charged and commanded to be aiding and assisting to the Civil Power in the Quelling & Suppressing any Riots, Tumults & other Disorders" that might occur during the trial. While many settlers in both New Jersey and Pennsylvania perceived all Indian peoples as a threat and danger to their communities, New Jersey appeared to be more successful in maintaining civil control over local vigilantes.[5]

Those in Pennsylvania sympathetic to their own Indian neighbors interpreted Governor Belcher's actions as a commitment to protecting noncombatant Indians, and rightly viewing this as a sign that New Jersey was a safer haven than William Penn's colony. In 1763, just months before the massacre of the Conestoga Indians, a community of pacifist Moravian Indians had escaped the retribution of the same group of Scots-Irish settlers by escaping first to Nazareth, a town several days' march north of Philadelphia. In November 1763 the Pennsylvania assembly decided that all 125 Indian refugees were to come to Philadelphia and subsequently housed them in the barracks at the government's expense. Nevertheless, even the assembly could not quell the demonstrations of hatred toward Indians that spilled into the streets of Penn's City of Brotherly Love. In response, colonial agents moved the refugees to Providence Island in the Delaware River, housing them in the same buildings used to quarantine sick sailors and passengers arriving from their Atlantic crossings. Other Native refugees from throughout Pennsylvania joined the Moravian group through the summer.

After the Paxton Boys had committed their gruesome murders of the Conestoga Indians in December 1763, they turned their vengeance on Philadelphia with a renewed wrath aimed at exterminating another pacifist Indian community. Even as Benjamin Franklin negotiated a temporary peace with this armed militia of backcountry citizens, the assembly took steps to remove the Indian refugees from the colony. In January 1764 this group, carrying papers guaranteeing their noncombatant status, crossed the Delaware River into New Jersey. Governor Belcher promised them safe passage through his colony on their way to what they hoped would be a final destination in upstate New York. Cadwallader Colden, governor of New York, did not share Belcher's sentiments and consequently refused the weary entourage entry to his colony.[6] A large group of refugee In-

Kindness Extended

dians entering his colony offered no foreseeable advantage to New York in these times of unrest, only more trouble. The governors and legislators of Pennsylvania, New Jersey, and New York struggled to maintain order, control lawlessness, and protect their citizens and properties throughout this era. Pennsylvania's government offered little protection and was unable to control its citizens. Government's official and unofficial solutions supported a policy of removal, exile, and internment. New York closed its borders to exiles and refused to aid Indian refugees from the war-torn areas of the other colonies. Governor Belcher, however, offered some asylum for select groups and implemented legislation meant to administratively identify, track, and control the noncombatant Indians living in New Jersey. Given these circumstances, it is easy to understand why Hannah Freeman crossed the Delaware River and found sanctuary in New Jersey.

Hannah and her kin spent seven years in exile. We cannot know whether they made this decision independently or whether they were encouraged to do so by their Quaker neighbors. It is likely that Hannah and her kin settled somewhere near the Quaker stronghold of Woodbury, a farming community that had once been within Penn's original colonial boundary and was situated almost directly across the Delaware River from the Brandywine Lenape lands.[7] The Quaker residents of Woodbury had many ties to the farmers along the Brandywine, and it is possible they arranged to provide Hannah and her family with support and protection during their sojourn there. It is also reasonable to suppose that Hannah and her relatives settled into a similar pattern of work and residence within this agricultural community. Perhaps other Indian families in New Jersey who lived along the rivers and creeks that cut inland from the Delaware River opened their homes to their fellow Lenapes and distant kin. Alternatively, it is conceivable Hannah and her kin boarded with their employers or took up residence in available cabins, just as so many other itinerant workers did. Speculation is all we have on this point. Hannah's recollection of this period of her life, as she presented it to Moses Marshall in 1797, offered no details about her exile in New Jersey. What is certain is that Hannah Freeman and her family left the Brandywine River valley in 1763 due to the murders of the Conestoga community by the Paxton Boys. And what is equally certain is that they returned seven years later to reclaim their homes in southeastern Pennsylvania without any objections from the Quaker residents who asserted ownership of the Lenape lands.

Hannah saw little physical change in the Brandywine River valley when she returned from exile. The county continued to be a highly productive agricultural region that, despite new waves of immigrants, remained firmly in the hands of English Quakers. In that regard, nothing had changed during those years of exile. The families she knew still lived in their stone farmhouses, worked in the endless fields of flax and rye that covered the rolling hills, and prayed in their simple meetinghouses scattered throughout the region. Hannah and her kin—her grandmother Jane, her mother, Sarah, her aunts Nanny and Betty—seamlessly returned to their routines so abruptly ended seven years earlier. They resettled in their cabins near Kennett and Centre, and appeared to return to their seasonal occupations working among the local farmers and tending their own gardens, livestock, and homes. The number of Hannah's employers increased to include William Brinton, a member of one of the first families of Chester County.[8] He owned large estates throughout the region, including a mill situated on the Brandywine River that overlooked one of the major fords in the river. Like most Quaker families, the Brintons were related to the Webbs, Marshalls, and Pierces through marriage, and it is most likely that these same Quaker kinship ties provided Hannah Freeman and her family many of the same benefits they formerly enjoyed in their Lenape communities. The Quaker kinship networks offered protection and economic opportunities for Hannah and her relatives to earn wages that supplemented their own small homesteads. In addition, perhaps most critical to the perseverance of Hannah's Lenape kin was the fact that no one in the region impeded her family's access to its lands along the Brandywine River, even after seven years in exile. Some observed her riding her horse up and down the banks of the Brandywine acting as though she "was the queen of the whole neighborhood."[9]

In the 1770s Hannah's world seemed encapsulated between the physical boundaries of three Quaker meetings and the interwoven relationships of their membership: the Kennett, Birmingham, and Centre meetings. Most of the Quakers who were a part of her life were also members of these three meetings, and all three meetings drew their core memberships from families who now claimed ownership of the lands guaranteed to Checochinican and the Brandywine Lenapes by William Penn.[10] It is important to understand how deeply Hannah's neighbors understood their obligation to the Brandywine Lenapes. From one generation to the next, the Quaker families who knew Hannah Freeman and the Brandywine Lenapes expressed a continuing sense of obligation that is impossible to ignore. This network of Quaker support mirrored and extended many of the benefits that the Lenapes' internal kinship ties had provided in an earlier era. Hannah and her family thus returned to find little changed in this corner of rural southeastern Pennsylvania. Their cabins and gardens only needed tending and care before old routines were established. Within a short time Chester County residents soon saw these familiar Lenape faces going about the business of living just as they had before 1763.

Hannah Freeman was a hardworking and independent woman. As had been true of generations of Lenape women before her, she had a great capacity throughout her lifetime to adapt to constantly changing economic opportunities. When Europeans made first contact with Lenape people in the Delaware River valley, the women increased their production of corn and textiles in part to satisfy the growing demand for these items by Swedish and English settlers. They adapted ancient skills used in the production of indigenous textiles to the modern world of cloth manufacturing. Later, Lenape women sought new economic opportunities and found a market for wolf skins, the predators being a bane of local farmers. They also continued to fine-tune their agricultural and textile production to take advantage of settler interests. Hannah thus inherited a legacy of entrepreneurialism. She crossed into new territory, but she retained old knowledge—and both would serve her well. Each generation of Lenape women encountered changes that led to adaptations. Hannah's grandmothers cooked in metal pots rather than clay, and her mother wore skirts made of cotton rather than animal hides. Hannah adapted as well: she learned to spin flax and tend pigs, she spoke English, and she earned wages, all signs of modernity. Too often these changes and adaptations are perceived as indications of acculturation or assimilation, indications that she and other Native women were losing their Indianness, as if that were a threadbare dress handed down from generation to generation. Rather than loss of culture, I would argue that Hannah's ability to adapt to a new way of living was perhaps the most salient proof of her Lenape identity. The history of her people, a story of migration and change, was also a story of new communities and new people. Hannah Freeman's seamless return to her former home not only reaffirmed her identity as a Lenape woman in an increasingly non-Native world, it also identified the Brandywine River valley as something more complicated than a Quaker community. Her return was a clear indication that the river valley still belonged to the Brandywine Lenapes, and local Quakers' acquiescence to her return was further confirmation.[11]

Hannah continued to work for many of the same families as before her exile. At the Chandler farm she earned wages largely through sewing. After her return from exile, she was more often employed sewing in Quaker households than any other task and earned the majority of her wages doing this work. Besides money, she was also paid for her labor in "sheets of good cloth."[12]

Kindness Extended

Like her grandmother's, Hannah's working life was adapted to a seasonal calendar. In the winter she worked for local farmers earning wages, room, and board by spinning and sewing. At night she continued to make traditional Lenape baskets from wood splints and reeds that she would later sell throughout the region. Local residents recalled that after a long day's work for their families, Hannah sat by the warmth and light of the fireplace and wove baskets. Some recalled that she occasionally smoked a pipe, creating an unforgettable image. In the summer months they recalled her traveling throughout the region selling the products of her winter labors, sometimes on horseback but most often on foot.[13]

During the warmer seasons Hannah turned her attention to her own homestead. Most often she spent her time at the same family cabin on William Webb's property in which she had been born. Close to the cabin she had a small orchard and garden where she grew corn, herbs, and other foods. She caught fish and turtles, part of the traditional Lenape diet, from local streams. One local writer in his recollections about Hannah was repulsed by the idea of turtles as food, deeming it a "savage" behavior.[14] While Hannah relied on the knowledge of generations of Lenape farmers to remain relatively self-sufficient, she also expanded her agricultural expertise to include livestock. Hannah owned several pigs and cows that she herded to local farms during the winter months. This indicates that her diet included smoke meats and dairy, European foods that had only recently been added to the Lenapes' regimen. When Hannah arrived to work for local farmers, they expected her small collection of livestock as well. The farmers who relied on outside labor, as most did, accounted for the material needs of their workers by subtracting it either from their wages or from the goods that were often part of their compensation. Not only did the live-in laborers need room and board, they also required shoes, clothes, and sometimes medicine and doctors.[15] No doubt part of Hannah's expenses included the cost of keeping her animals unless, as in so many other circumstances, her Quaker employers did not expect repayment because of their consciousness of an older set of obligations. In the summer Hannah was known to cross the fields with her pigs and dogs in tow. Chester County residents remembered that the pigs and the dogs both responded to her commands. It is imperative that we look beyond the "quaint" aspect of these local memories about Indian peoples. Such stories and recollections form an important, though limited, body of evidence that provides some glimpse into the lives of indigenous peoples who chose to remain on their ancestral homelands. Too often such accounts are dismissed as local legends, myths, and folklore—and real stories of survival, struggle, and cultural persistence are lost. These stories of Hannah Freeman in Chester County are more than picturesque images of a local curiosity. Hannah's small collection of livestock, her constant employment and the success of her own farmstead, even after a seven-year exile, indicate that she was an economically stable and independent woman and continued to be so for most of her life. She was not dependent on her Quaker neighbors as a lifelong charity case, nor does her life provide evidence of a failed race or culture.[16]

Hannah's transition from exile to the Brandywine River valley was smooth, but the remainder of the decade was to include some of the most difficult struggles of her life. Once again Chester County residents witnessed a war that brought violence and chaos to Hannah's doorstep. The final quarter of the eighteenth century is familiar turf for those interested in American history. It is hard not to see every event and person caught in a web of inevitability that culminates in the American Revolution and the founding of the United States. But, not unlike the lives of so many nameless individuals who made up the majority of this colonial population, Hannah Freeman's story does not play a significant role in the history of the American Revolution or the founding of the nation. There was a time when what we knew about the American Revolution was understood only through the experiences of statesmen and generals, treatises and proclamations. Today we have a more holistic understanding of the impact of the war because we ask better questions, particularly about the experiences of women, the poor, slaves, and indigenous peoples. But perhaps the most neglected and difficult stories left to tell are the experiences of Native American women during the colonial era. There are a few accounts of Native women who fought alongside their husbands during the war. One remarkable story is about Tyonajanegen, an Oneida woman who took to the battlefield with pistols blazing in support of her people's efforts to defeat the British. Other stories tell of the exceptional heroism of women who rose to be negotiators of peace, like the Ghigau (Beloved Woman) of the Cherokee Nation. Stories like these tell of extraordinary actions, but there are few accounts of indigenous women during this era that go beyond their exceptional roles or their anonymous victimization.[17] Hannah and her family experienced the French and Indian War as exiles from their own country, but when the American Revolution came to the Brandywine River valley, Hannah bore some witness to events that played out on her own lands.

In early September 1777 twenty-nine thousand British and American soldiers marched north toward the Brandywine River at the height of the harvesting season. General William Howe's British forces, supplemented by four thousand to five thousand German Hessians, marched north with the intention of capturing Philadelphia, the seat of the revolutionary government. As General Howe marched north, George Washington, commander of the Continental army, moved his regiments to the east side of the Brandywine River on lands Hannah Freeman considered her own. The marquis de Lafayette, participating in his first American engagement, seized the home of one of Hannah's regular employers, Gideon Gilpin, to serve as his headquarters. On September 11, 1777, the battle of the Brandywine played out in the fields and forests where Hannah lived and worked. At the end of the day Washington was forced to retreat north and east of the Brandywine River in hopes of making another stand. Ultimately the Continental army failed to defend the city, and the revolutionary government abandoned Philadelphia, fleeing west to Lancaster to avoid capture. Howe and his British regiments spent their winter enjoying the comforts of the largest city in the British colonies while Washington and his poorly supplied regiments spent their winter at Valley Forge.[18]

The battle of Brandywine was a short-lived event, but the direct impact of the war on local residents lingered for some time afterward. Washington's strategy focused on preventing the British from crossing the river at four major points along the river, including Brinton's Ford, a short walk from Hannah's homestead on William Webb's property. While we do not know exactly where she was the day of the battle, it is certain that she was working in the area "at the time when the soldiers were about."[19] As Washington led his regiments in a retreat in order to take another stand at defending Philadelphia, Howe and the British forces remained in the area for another week. Neither Hannah nor her neighbors participated directly in the fighting. Local Quakers for the most part remained committed to the peace testimony even as fighting occurred in and around their meetinghouses in Chester County and did not take up arms on one side or the other. But the demands of a large army are great, and local farmers raised little resistance when soldiers plundered their barns, springhouses, and homes during and after the battle. Because the battle occurred at the peak of harvest season, Howe was able to readily resupply and replenish his more than ten thousand soldiers before they reengaged Washington's troops. Gideon Gilpin later filed a claim for losses in the aftermath of the battle: "10 milch cows, 1 yoke of oxen, 48 sheep, 28 swine, 12 tons of hay, 230 bushels of wheat, 50 pounds of bacon," and more. He was just one farmer among many who eventually filed claims; the complete list establishes not only the wartime demands of a fighting army but also the wealth of Chester County's farmers. The losses claimed in the postwar years were so great that three of Chester County's townships were exempt from taxes for several years. Although many of the local Quaker farmers were reluctant to support the war, they willingly opened their homes and meetinghouses to the sick and wounded on both sides of the fight. Birmingham and Kennett meetinghouses were not only sites of some of the day's firefights, they also served as places of refuge for the wounded and dying, with local residents caring for both. Members of the Birmingham Meeting buried unidentified British and American soldiers in a common grave near the graves of their own families. It is very likely that Hannah was there side by side with her neighbors, perhaps tending to the sick or feeding soldiers, or perhaps just continuing her daily work around the disruptions and chaos the battle brought to the region. We do know that her Quaker neighbors did not endorse or support the American Revolution, and at the war's end they struggled to find their place in the new United States. But we can never know how Hannah perceived this war or if she understood the immediate ramifications of the war's outcome for all Indian peoples.[20]

In 1783 the British signed the Treaty of Paris with the United States, in which they abandoned all claims to the thirteen colonies. Hannah's Quaker friends, neighbors, and benefactors were divested of their identity as British subjects and, reluctantly or not, acknowledged their new status as citizens of the United States. Hannah's identity, however, remained constant: she was born a Lenape and she remained one, despite the contestations of empires old and new. It is unlikely that Hannah gave any thought to the events and debates that dominate the historical narrative of this period. From her perspective, she was simply witnessing another round of war, death, and destruction, an all too familiar pattern in the "peaceable kingdom." As James Madison, Benjamin Franklin, and Pennsylvania's own John Dickinson debated the terms of the American Constitution and its amendments in nearby Philadelphia, the future of one Lenape woman was not their concern. They struggled over the many meanings of democracy and representation and wrestled with an array of ideas about expansion, borders, and boundaries. But the founding fathers and the authors of the new Republic's governing documents gave scant consideration to the indigenous peoples living within the boundaries of their new nation. Whether allies or enemies during the revolution or before, Native Americans were excluded from any discussions of citizenship or property rights. Their independence, identities, and cultures were subsumed to an economic status relegated to the "commerce clause," which continues to grant Congress vast powers over American Indians and their nations.[21] In the years after the Treaty of Paris, the new nation's policy makers learned very quickly that Native Americans never endorsed their capitulation.

Native American peoples living throughout the new boundaries of the United States continued to counter the forces of dispossession in order to preserve their own homelands, formulating new approaches in their own efforts to promote peaceful cohabitation with a growing settler population. War decided the boundaries proclaimed and ceded by distant allies and enemies, but the day-to-day interactions of Lenapes, Shawnees, Munsees, Mohawks, and so many others were more complicated than we might suspect. For generations the close cohabitation of settlers and their indigenous neighbors led to complex exchanges exhibited not only in the larger, public arenas of diplomacy but also in the daily lives of individuals like Hannah Freeman and her Quaker neighbors. Generally these exchanges were situated in conflicting views of land tenure: English-based notions of delineated boundaries, individual ownership, and all the attendant rights suggested by that ownership versus Native ideas of property rights based on kinship, resources, and a fluidity of boundaries and use. Native leaders like Joseph Brant (Mohawk) and Hendrick Aupaumut (Mohican) proposed divergent diplomatic solutions to preserve their own collective communities in the aftermath of the American Revolution and used the written

Kindness Extended

word to articulate, define, and map Native space rather than capitulate to the exclusive authority of colonial negotiators.[22] At the same time, there were many locations where those divergent concepts of land tenure were negotiated in the day-to-day exchanges between neighbors. The ongoing negotiations and renegotiations between Hannah Freeman and her Quaker neighbors in Chester County provide a different way of understanding the cultural exchanges that took place on the most intimate level. They had mutual interests in protecting and preserving their homelands, though they perceived and interpreted those spaces very differently in the years after the war. Before long the Native and settler residents of Chester County had settled into a seasonal rhythm that satisfied most of its inhabitants. Within a few years the dependable bounty of southeastern Pennsylvania allowed Quaker farmers to rebound and recover. Before long Chester County's scars of war faded from view.

In the years following the war, Hannah Freeman seemed to share in the prosperity that her neighbors in Chester County enjoyed. She had plenty of work of her own choosing that provided her with money and materials, affording her economic comfort and stability. Whether she was walking from one farm to the other selling her baskets and brooms or riding her horse through the woods, Hannah Freeman was a familiar sight to all who lived in the area. The memories of Chester County Quakers are embedded with images of Hannah in a variety of settings and relationships that when woven together provide a vital portrait of a Lenape woman in the eighteenth century. Hannah's small homestead, though well known to most of her neighbors, still afforded her some seclusion and protection from strangers or passersby. She participated in the local economy, making purchases that were not unlike those of her colonial neighbors. Hannah purchased a load of "good hay" for her animals from Richard Barnard and paid him 400 shillings for the delivery. Later Barnard also noted deliveries of firewood, bushels of apples, and gallons of cider water, a nonfermented beverage that was much preferred to water in the colonial era. According to Marshall Swayne, his family remembered that Hannah was obstinate about her economic relationship with her neighbors, refusing to accept any charity and insisting on paying in kind or cash for anything she received, even if her neighbors tried to refuse the payment. Hannah's economic prosperity is also evident in some of her material acquisitions. Some of her closest Quaker neighbors remembered that Hannah prized a set of silver spoons that she had acquired at some point in her life. She relied on her neighbors to keep her spoons and other valuables safe "when going on a journey to visit her relations," suggesting not only a level of vulnerability but also a level of trust she shared with local Quakers.[23]

Hannah's visibility in Chester County after the American Revolution is cited as evidence of her assimilation into colonial culture and her increased dependence on the charity of her Quaker neighbors.[24] However, the same stories that are referenced as evidence of her acculturation also provide glimpses into an ancient Lenape way of life that continued to be a very tangible part of her identity and prosperity. As a Lenape woman, her independent lifestyle, production of food and material goods for subsistence and exchange, ownership of livestock, and participation in a woman-centered network of kinship are not evidence of abrupt change; instead they indicate a consistent adaptation of old practices to new opportunities. At the same time, Hannah and other Indian people, hiding in plain sight of their colonial neighbors, engaged in practices and activities that were uniquely their own. Most obvious of these are Hannah's knowledge of indigenous medicine and her continued cultivation and application of these natural medicines. Other local residents remembered numerous small settlements of several wigwams and cabins occupied by local Lenape families who, like Hannah, found ways to stay in their ancient homelands. More than one farmer recalled that these small Lenape groups built their homes along creeks and drainages, often on hillsides with southern exposures, a settlement pattern archaeologists recognize as indicative of Lenape culture centuries earlier. Hannah continued to weave fishing nets from wild grapevines to make the most of this local resource and preserved and stored her catch in the same manner as generations of Lenape women had before her. John Parker, whose children Hannah treated, recalled that Indian women "in considerable numbers" gathered annually at a particular tract of land in the county during several months of the year to engage in basket weaving as a community.[25] In the fall these same groups of women were spotted working together, helping each other during harvest, pounding roots, and stringing corn on poles in order to preserve their crops for the winter to come.

On a more personal note, some neighbors recalled what they perceived as her "primitive" and "superstitious" eccentricities, which may well have been no more eccentric than their Quaker belief that an invisible spirit inhabited their bodies.[26] Some remembered that Hannah refused to eat after sunset, and others told of her great respect for the thunder that came with the spring and late summer storms. Thunder beings are deities second only to the creator and the keepers of the four directions. The Lenapes believed the *pethakoweyuk* were responsible for watering the earth and also had the power to fight the great horned serpent and other monsters that lived beneath the water.[27] Hannah's continued respect for that invisible power and her ongoing practices and beliefs in a Lenape way of life are evident in the close details and recollections of those who knew her. However, their perceptions, rooted in a racialized history of contact and interaction with Native Americans, skewed their understanding of Hannah's life. Her determined and persistent claims to the Brandywine River valley is powerful evidence of her unwavering Lenape identity despite the overwhelming pulls of colonial culture that surrounded and enveloped her ancient homeland. In life, in ceremony, and in death, Hannah Freeman and her kin remained Lenapes.

Just as Hannah Freeman and her extended family finally began to experience some level of peace, stability, and security, a series of personal tragedies struck at the core of the Lenape-centered world in which she flourished. In 1775 Hannah's grandmother Jane died. As the oldest member of Hannah's extended family, Jane most likely served as clan mother, teacher, and ceremonial leader to a kinship network of Lenapes throughout the region. Hannah's grandmother's death was followed by the death of her aunt Betty around 1780. At the time of their deaths neither woman lived with Hannah along the Brandywine. Her grandmother died "near Schuylkill," a river that was once home to a dense population of Lenape communities. Lenape lands associated with the Schuylkill, Brandywine, and "forks" of the Delaware River were hard-fought strongholds of Lenape lands prior to the French and Indian War, but in the last decades of the eighteenth century only small enclaves of extended families like Hannah's remained. At the time of Betty's death, she lived with her husband and several female family members along Chester Creek, halfway between the Brandywine and the Schuylkill rivers. Some local residents who remember Betty and her husband believed that she was buried in a Lenape cemetery not far from their home.[28]

There seemed to be little change in Hannah's life after the deaths of her grandmother and aunt, but in such a small, interdependent, woman-centered community it is easy to imagine that the kin they left behind sorely felt the loss of the elder women. Nora Thompson Dean, a modern Lenape woman from Oklahoma, vividly recalled how her own mother passed down ceremonies, special knowledge, and "women's stories" that were part of a very old tradition and a rich vault of wisdom specific to Lenape heritage and ancestral homelands. As a young girl Nora learned her gender-specific role in the Big House ceremony, a central spiritual event for the Lenape peoples. There were dances, practices, and responsibilities for women and girls that both eighteenth-century Hannah and twentieth-century

Nora learned from their grandmothers, aunts, and mothers. Although these practices and ceremonies changed over time, their meaning and purpose bound these women together over generations and were central to their identity as Lenape women. When she reached "physical maturity," Nora's female relatives conducted a coming-of-age ceremony that was ancient in its origins. In centuries past the event was celebrated through a period of isolation, prayer, and cleansing that took place in a bark house set apart from the others. In twentieth-century Oklahoma, much had changed in the Lenape way of life, so her aunts and mother improvised by turning the family living room into a separate ceremonial space where Nora could experience the same ceremonies as Hannah and generations of Lenape women before her.[29]

At the heart of this time-honored passage was the significance of the ceremony, not the extraneous conditions of the event. As part of this passage her mother gave away all of Nora's childhood clothes and toys to mark the end of childhood. (Nora recalled that her mother was easy on her, letting her keep a favorite doll.) Nora was instructed not to touch her face or her hair; her mother wrapped her hands with cloth "in case I forgot." Nora's mother made all new clothes for her, including longer skirts and "even new earrings." But the significance of the ceremony was not in the clothes or the jewelry but in the knowledge that was shared from one generation of Lenape women to the next. "My mother spent a great deal of time with me," teaching Nora that her childhood was behind her and that there were new things and new responsibilities she had to learn. Her mother took her into the woods, sharing knowledge about plants and the many purposes they served, including the sap of the wild grapevine, which "would make my hair grow long—as long as the grapevine—and keep it from getting white" when she grew old. Nora's mother taught her to wash her face and gargle with the icy water from the winter streams to preserve her good health. Nora recalled that her mother explained that she was "being very easy on me" because in earlier times they had to jump in the water for a swim "to keep them healthy and make them tough." More than one Quaker neighbor who shared their recollections of the Lenape and Hannah recounted seeing Lenape women dunk their babies in cold stream water to encourage their good health. Nora also recalled that for the most part her mother and extended family did not go to "white" doctors but relied on "Indian herbal medicines." In her new role as a Lenape woman, Nora learned "to do the work the women did. I pounded corn into meal using a *kohokan* [mortar] until my hands were blistered." She recalled that the old women told her they listened for "the sound of the pounding corn" to find out which girl was the hardest worker, as her effort was a reflection of her character and maturity. These observations allowed the elder Lenape women to arrange marriages between the best-suited younger members of their community. Nora recalled that both her grandmother and mother entered marriages that were determined by their families in ceremonies that were conducted according to Lenape traditions. At the ceremony the community gathered to witness the event, which was led by an elder. There were no vows exchanged or licenses signed. Instead, blessings were offered by the community and the elder leader finalized the union by wrapping one long strand of white wampum over their heads and around their necks, proclaiming them husband and wife.[30]

Whether experienced in the small enclaves of eighteenth-century Pennsylvania or the homesteads of twentieth-century Oklahoma, the heart of Lenape culture and identity beat strongly in the wisdom and knowledge of their women and in a continuity of traditions that were externally altered and adapted to new circumstances as their history demanded but remained constant in their lessons. Many of those same intrinsic values and worldviews sustained Hannah Freeman throughout her life because she was part of a vibrant network of Lenape women. Dispossession, violence, warfare, and expansion altered and changed her people and their communities throughout her lifetime, but through all of those experiences, her grandmothers, aunts, and mother provided a strong foundation for Hannah to create and sustain an independent and successful life under nearly insurmountable pressures. And while Hannah did find ways of weaving Quaker men and women into this network of community, her world revolved around those female Lenape kin.[31]

In 1785 Hannah Freeman's world was unalterably changed by the death of her mother, Sarah, followed closely by her only other maternal aunt, Nanny. At the time of Sarah's death, she and Hannah were both working and living on Swithin Chandler's farm in Centre, Delaware. The Chandlers were lifelong friends of the Brandywine Lenapes and knew Hannah and her kin very well. While we do not know the circumstances of Sarah's death, local residents recalled that her funeral was an event to be remembered. Members of the Pennock family remembered that Sarah's body was carried from Centre to the Marshall farm, where it was buried in a traditional Lenape ceremony and cemetery. There were a number of well-known Lenape cemeteries throughout Chester County that local residents understood to be in continuing use by Lenapes living in the area. The family cemetery of Hannah's kin was situated on the property formerly owned by Abraham Marshall, part of the same tract sold by Nathaniel Newlin, contested by Checochinican, and close to the "deep woods" Hannah Freeman called home. Sarah's body was carried from Centre to Newlin, a journey of approximately fifteen miles, to a final resting place marked by a stand of ancient trees, not far from the Lenapes' beloved Brandywine River. There are no accounts of who attended the procession or of the burial ceremony, but in 1785 such an event as this was unheard of in this busy, heavily populated corner of southeastern Pennsylvania.[32]

It is important to reflect on other traditions that were probably a part of this event. From the first encounters between Lenape and Europeans in the seventeenth century to the modern day, observers have noted the particular care the Lenape people took in the burial of their kin. Most likely Hannah and other women prepared Sarah for burial by washing her body and dressing her in clothes that were specially selected for this passage. She might have been adorned with jewelry and painted red with specific patterns reserved for this occasion. Some personal affects may have been placed in the coffin, perhaps family heirlooms, tools, or other objects symbolic of her life and her clan. Male members of her family and community carried Sarah's coffin, as Hannah and other mourners followed the procession. It is not known whether any Quaker friends walked in this procession, especially given their own rejection of overt religious rituals, but nothing prevented their attendance. Quaker funerary practices were quite different from Native ones. Burials were simple events, with the emphasis on remembrance of the life lived, not mourning loss.[33] The disposition of the body after death was not nearly as important to Quakers as it was to Lenapes, who believed in a physical resurrection after death. Lenape burial practices centered on specific rituals and an extended mourning period. The twelve-day ceremonial period culminated when the deceased was finally placed in the grave. At the gravesite the coffin was placed in the ground with the head to the east. Before closing the coffin, those conducting the ceremony made a small hole in it, close to the head, that allowed the soul to depart when it left the body. There are variations in descriptions of this practice, but the fundamentals are consistent over centuries. The Lenape believe in an afterlife, and burial ceremonies and practices are meant to help their kin find the spirit world. The burial ceremony concluded with a feast in which the family shared food with mourners, leaving food for the deceased as well.[34] What a scene for the ages this gathering of mourners might have presented to a traveler passing by that day. Lenape men, women, and children standing alongside a scattering of local Quakers on a small hill overlooking the Brandywine River, some remembering one woman's life and others remembering so much more. Our shared histories are illustrated with images of treaties, warriors, and important men engaged in conflict and awash with hostilities and violence not forgotten. How different would this story of our shared pasts be if there were more accounts like this of our common humanity?

Hannah's close circle of female kin soon lost another member. The winter after her mother's death, Hannah went to "her Aunt Nanny and Staid all winter."[35] Nanny lived in Concord, less than five miles from Hannah's Brandywine homestead. According to some sources, Hannah moved in with Nanny and her husband and possibly some other family members. Hannah's reason for moving in with her aunt is unclear. After her mother's death she may have felt a need to be close to her elderly aunt; perhaps she needed the support of her family as they mourned her mother's death. Lenape customs called for a period of mourning that could last for years. Whatever the reasons, her stay in Concord was short-lived. Nanny died sometime in the late 1780s. Some local residents who remembered Nanny and her family believed the elderly Lenape woman and her husband were buried in the local Quaker cemetery. It is not known what became of that part of Hannah's family, nor do we have any account of a funeral procession or of the events that marked Nanny's passing.

After the successive loss of her family members, Hannah returned to work, earning wages and in-kind payments as she had before her mother's death. What was different about her work at this time is that she was employed by one extended family for almost five years, rather than adhering to the more mobile pattern of previous years. During this period she worked exclusively for members of the Chandler family, who farmed the southern banks of the Brandywine River just over the border in Delaware. Although she continued to maintain her own home near the river, moving back and forth according to the seasons, for five years Hannah's working world was more fixed than before. It is easy to translate this fixed employment as a sign of economic stability, but it might also suggest that fewer local farmers were interested in hiring her. Fortunately, she continued to be paid wages equivalent to those of other women laborers in the region. The Chandlers had a long history with Hannah and the Brandywine Lenapes—a history, perhaps, that they were less likely to forget than some of their other neighbors. Another factor that might account for the limited number of employers is that Hannah's circle of female kin and network of support was greatly decreased. How many other Lenape women were walking the paths and roads of Chester County seeking work or selling their baskets by the 1790s? Were the changes around her and the loss of close kin causing Hannah to reevaluate her "usual way of living"?[36] Hannah was not the only person in Chester County experiencing alterations in her daily life. Her Quaker and non-Quaker neighbors alike witnessed great changes at the end of the eighteenth century that had a lasting impact on all of their lives.

As the new nation struggled to govern the former thirteen colonies, the postwar period proved to be economically volatile for many of its new citizens. Many families and soldiers displaced in the aftermath of the war looked for new opportunities to acquire land and find employment. Some of those individuals gravitated to urban areas like Philadelphia for work and charity, while others took to the roads that threaded the rich farmlands and small towns of the new nation hoping for a better life. Before long many of these seekers looked to the western lands, now occupied by their former Indian neighbors and Indian nations they did not know. Southeastern Pennsylvania, like other economically vibrant regions in the new Republic, experienced the pains and prosperity of growth and expansion in ways that occasionally reflected William Penn's legacy but most often responded to the demands of its citizens and the marketplace. By the 1790s Quakers in southeastern Pennsylvania were finding new ways to participate in the nation's political future, while closer to home they continued to dominate local financial and government agencies.

In 1795 members of the Philadelphia Yearly Meeting, the governing body of Pennsylvania's various Quaker congregations, organized the Committee for the Improvement and Civilization of the Indian, later known as the Indian Committee. The objectives of the organization were both diplomatic and missionary. Building on the legacy of William Penn and the Quaker role in Indian negotiations since the end of the French and Indian War, the committee members asserted their interest in national politics in a way that was compatible with Quaker convictions. Members of the Indian Committee were indispensable to federal agents and officers who sought to acquire new Indian lands from the Appalachians to the Mississippi River. At the same time, Quakers funded and implemented a series of missionary activities beginning with the Oneidas in New York. Chester County sent numerous missionaries to the newly acquired territories from western New York to Ohio, Indiana, and beyond. Quakers, armed with blind assumptions about the superiority of their own way of life, hoped to "save" the Indians from extinction. While some Quaker missionaries set up model farms in distant territories, others returned home with Indian children to educate and influence.[37] Local Quakers throughout Chester County temporarily "adopted" Indian children from western Pennsylvania, New York, and Ohio to work on their farms and in their businesses and homes. After training the children were sent home again to further the cause of "civilization." None of Hannah's employers housed Indian children, but it is easy to imagine what Hannah might have thought had she met young Shawnee or Miami children working in her neighbors' homes and shops. Nevertheless, Quakers' diplomatic expertise and missionary efforts proved successful from their perspective. They played an indispensable role in the federal government's programs to dispossess all Native Americans east of the Mississippi River of their lands, and their early Indian "education" efforts became one model for the Indian boarding school program that later destroyed so many Indian families.

While Quakers from Chester County involved themselves in the future of Indian peoples and the acquisition of their western lands, other leaders of their community lent their expertise and civic commitments to another equally pressing problem facing the new Republic: poverty. The poor placed new burdens on county, township, and municipal governments. In earlier times no systematic program or agency offered relief to the poor and sick. Beginning in the early eighteenth century Chester County collected a tax for the relief of the poor and appointed overseers to determine eligibility based on residence and need. Once the overseer made the determination, the "deserving poor" received money to alleviate their destitute condition. Because of the ad hoc administration of the relief, there were many disputes over who was entitled to the funds and which township was responsible. Whether inspired by Quaker ethics or because of its proximity to the largest cities in the United States, by the 1790s Chester County found its coffers and constituents stressed by the needs of the poor.

As Chester County politicians struggled to come to terms with the burden of caring for the indigent members of their community, Hannah Freeman faced a new set of challenges. By the mid-1790s Hannah was not well. After her aunt Nanny's death, she did not immediately return to her own homestead near the river but took up a more permanent residence with some of her previous employers. Initially she moved to Kennett and went to work for William Webb; she "worked for her board sometimes but got no money." Next she spent three years at Sam Levi's, "where she made her home and worked sometime." While her lengthy stays with one family at a time were similar to her years with the Chandlers, there was a major difference: Hannah did not receive wages for her work, only room and board. Also, unlike the other accounts of her working life, there are no details of what she did except that she made "baskets, besoms &c."[38] There is no mention of the numerous activities previously noted by her neighbors. Richard Barnard no longer delivered hay for

Kindness Extended

her animals nor wood for her fireplace. She was no longer seen herding her small but lively entourage of livestock to graze in local fields. Neighbors no longer spotted her riding her horse along the river's banks.

Those neighbors and friends who knew Hannah Freeman and the history of the Brandywine Lenape were instrumental in determining the policies and laws that institutionalized poor relief in Chester County. For decades they treated Hannah as friend and neighbor, perhaps in some cases as a member of their extended families. She reciprocated those bonds, as her mother, aunts, and grandmothers had before her. But in 1797 Moses Marshall ended that lifelong relationship with the stroke of his pen when he and his neighbors took the first steps to institutionalize Hannah Freeman as an indigent. Although the administrative process of her "Examination" acknowledged her lifelong residency in the area, it permanently erased her claims to the lands guaranteed by William Penn's treaty with Checochinican's people. The "Kindness Extended" created in 1798 formalized her neighbors' contractual obligations to provide funds, room, and board for her care and removed any trace of doubt of Hannah's status in their community.[39] All thirty-four Quaker men who gathered together in Richard Barnard's house to sign the contract understood that Hannah Freeman did not have long to live. The plans for the poorhouse were under way, and its construction on the lands claimed by the Brandywine Lenapes could not have escaped their notice. If Hannah died before its completion, the funds provided would cover the expense of her burial. Whether Hannah's life ended in one of their homes or in the newly built poorhouse did not alter the fact that her death ended the Lenapes' legal claim to the lands along the Brandywine River. From the perspective of her Quaker neighbors, Hannah's life was testimony to the legacy of William Penn and Quaker benevolence toward the Indians, and her death closed the book on any Lenape claims to the Brandywine River valley.

CHAPTER SIX

The Betrayal

On November 12, 1800, Hannah Freeman walked through the front doors of the newly built Chester County Alms House. The smell of fresh lumber and the sounds of ongoing construction filled the air as she climbed the stairs and passed through the hall to meet the waiting directors. Across the field, work was already beginning on the potter's field where those who died as inmates were to be buried. Joseph Cope, David Denny, John Marshall, and Nathaniel Walker sat behind the table with pens poised, ready to accept the poor from nineteen townships throughout the county.[1] All these commissioners were familiar with Hannah's case, but not all knew her personally. They recorded the name, age, race, township of residence, and date of admittance for each inmate in their oversized ledgers. One column remained empty: the final outcome of the case. For some, employment or a family member gained their release; for others, the final determination was death in the poorhouse. "Indian Hannah" was the first entry on the first page in the first admissions book for the Chester County Alms House.[2]

For generations, this entry would be used to declare that "Indian Hannah" was "the last of her kind" in Chester County and stand as documentary proof of Quaker benevolence toward Pennsylvania's original people. Despite Hannah's own use of Freeman as a surname, the recording director dismissed this part of her identity in favor of a colloquialism used to identify Indian people who lived in their colonial world. Her place of residence was listed as Newlin Township, a fact determined by

Moses Marshall's "examination" two years earlier. We cannot know what Hannah was thinking as she saw her name inscribed in the book or how she felt as the attendants led her to the upstairs room she was to occupy. It is not hard to imagine that at such a moment she reflected on the life she had lived and on the family and friends, past and present, who were part of her world. Did she see this as a temporary arrangement, one that would end when a neighbor or friend came forward to take her home, or did she know that her admittance was a permanent solution? Did Hannah Freeman know she would never go home again? For those who waited in line for admittance to the poorhouse, Hannah Freeman's arrival must have provoked some curiosity. There are no other Indian people listed in its entries. Some may have wondered who Hannah was. Perhaps they questioned why *she* was there?

For over a year Hannah remained a resident in the poorhouse. She witnessed the growth and expansion of the original building to include barns, a tannery, a smokehouse, and more. Inmates were required to work, with the exception of those who were ill or too young to do so. There were gardens to tend, laundry to do, food to prepare, and clothes to mend. Hannah was familiar with the day-to-day workings of a farm, but her regimented isolation as an inmate must have been difficult to cope with. Because she was old and ill, it is unlikely she was required to do daily work. If she was permitted or able to participate in some small way, it may have comforted her to be of use to this strange new community in which she lived. It is important to remember how fiercely independent Hannah Freeman was all of her life. However, if she remained in isolation, without the comfort of work or the company of others, then it is equally easy to see how her circumstances may have hastened her death.

On March 20, 1802, Hannah Freeman, member of the Turtle Clan and daughter of Checochinican's Brandywine Lenapes, died in the Chester County Alms House.[3] There is no record that a physician or any of her former friends or neighbors attended her final days. She was quickly buried in the western field designated as the poorhouse graveyard, contrary to her own wishes. Hannah Pierce, the wife of Jacob Pierce, one of her former benefactors, claimed Hannah as her friend and felt some regret that she failed to keep her promise to Hannah Freeman. Sometime before she was committed to the poorhouse, Hannah Freeman asked Pierce to promise that her body would rest in the Lenape burial ground not far from her former home and the Brandywine River. This was the same Lenape burial site that contained the graves of her mother and countless members of her clan and extended family. According to Pierce's recollections, Hannah Freeman died during harsh spring weather, and news of her death did not reach the Pierce family until some time after she had been interred in an unmarked grave in the potter's field. Pierce always felt some guilt that she had failed to fulfill Hannah Freeman's final request and was sorry that this Lenape women's life ended without notice or remembrance.[4]

Hannah Freeman did not lie quietly in her grave. The image of this tenacious Lenape woman represented many things to those who resurrected her in the decades after her death. Even before she breathed her last, Hannah Freeman was immortalized as the villainous Indian crone "Old Deb" in Charles Brockden Brown's novel *Edgar Huntley; or, Memoirs of a Sleepwalker.* According to literary scholar Andrew Newman, Brown's novel, published in 1799, is "one of the most frequently taught works of early American fiction." Newman persuasively argues that Brown crafted "Old Deb" from his own personal encounters with Hannah Freeman or from "hearsay, and perhaps acquaintance with a figure who had evidently captured the imagination of the residents of Chester County."[5]

Within a generation of her death, residents of Chester County repeatedly resurrected Hannah Freeman and betrayed the legacy and memory of the life she lived as their neighbor, friend, and heir to the treaty William Penn signed with the Brandywine Lenapes. In 1824 the *Village Record*, a local county newspaper, published a poem purportedly spoken over the grave of Hannah Freeman. The submission, penned by the anonymous "E," offered readers the fictive Indian voice of Outalissa, an "Indian Chief" returned "from the wilds of the west to visit the lands of his ancestors."[6] Outalissa offered the eulogy as a "last, sad requiem to the Lenape race." The poem is replete with images of brave and noble Lenapes succumbing to the white man's sword, "marked with livid stains," and their final, sad retreat into the west. While the poem focuses on the grander story of the vanishing Indian, Outalissa managed to remind readers that although her neighbors had known that Hannah's final wish was burial with her relatives, they had deliberately betrayed that promise and buried her in a potter's field on the poorhouse grounds. Outalissa expressed outrage that Hannah, the "last expiring stem" of the Lenapes, was laid to rest in "such a sad, last dwelling place." Speaking as one who had "vanished" into the west, the narrator of the poem lashed out at the destruction and wrongs that white Americans had committed against Indians of the eastern tribes and warned that the "Great Spirit" would return one day to rectify the violent past. Outalissa concluded the requiem with a comforting message that assured Chester County readers that no other Indians would come from the west "to wander pensive here." In his final stanza, Outalissa's reassurance turned ominous. He reminded the readers that as long as Indians lived, the memory of the wrongs committed against the Lenapes in Pennsylvania would not be forgotten. Not unlike Brown's Old Deb, E's Outalissa challenged the beatific construction of Penn's legacy that was already well under way.

The *Village Record* printed the poem because for the most part it was an overwhelmingly sentimental tribute to the "noble" Indians of the county's past. Remarkably, E felt compelled to offset Outalissa's darker themes and accusations by a strategically placed editorial comment, brief and to the point: Outalissa (fictive or real?) was wrong. According to E, the Native orator mistakenly confused the "Lenape with the whole body of Indians." Although the atrocities and devastation expressed in the poem had been experienced by the "general" Indian populations elsewhere, such was not the case in Pennsylvania. E attempted to quiet any disturbing thoughts the column's readers might have experienced by Outalissa's passionate warnings, declaring, "We all know that what might be termed the Pennsylvania Indians, part of whom was the Lenape tribe, were treated with comparative justice and humanity." The poem required this editorial because it spoke to larger national issues facing the new nation. Chester County's residents, though safely distanced from the hostilities endemic to westward expansion, were engaged in a national public dialogue concerning the solution of the ongoing "Indian problem." The same Chester County Quakers who initiated the sympathetic commemoration of the Lenapes were frontline witnesses to the emergence of pan-Indian resistance movements that marked the tumultuous beginning of the nineteenth century. Although most of these hostilities took place west of the Appalachians, Quaker missionaries and diplomats alike played pivotal roles, and all felt the impact of the resultant policies and politics. By 1820 the massive westward deportations of Indian peoples from east of the Mississippi River began in earnest, continuing into the second half of the century. The often-expressed idea of the vanishing Indian became national policy with the Indian Removal Act of 1832, and the public conscience wrestled with the issue. Pennsylvanians entered into this public discourse assured that William Penn's legacy as a humanitarian and friend of the Indians relieved them of any direct responsibility for the current injustice facing Indian nations.

Hannah's story surfaced again in the Chester County press concurrent with the Cherokee removal. In 1839 the *Register and Examination* published an extended story by "I.M.," a resident of Newlin, that illustrated the schizophrenic nature of the state's public memory and the problems inherent in achieving reconciliation in a narrative of "benevolent and peaceful" conquest and extinction. The story began as a recollection of a summer outing during which the author visited the "hut" of Hannah Freeman located "beside a beautiful spring in a dense wood . . . the most wild and secluded in the whole neighborhood."[7] The experience led I.M. to recall in great detail the story of Hannah's life. I.M. emphasized the kindness of local residents as she lent yet another voice to the "last of her kind" refrain. The reporter relayed anecdotes that portrayed Hannah as childlike and an object of pity. She amused readers with comical images of Hannah with her dogs and Hannah bewildered by the "witchcraft" at work in a compass. She condescendingly compared Hannah's naiveté to that of the Arawak Indians whom Columbus claimed he duped by predicting an eclipse of the moon. I.M. alternated such amusing recollections with images that evoked shame and remorse: Hannah as "last remnant," as "destitute," as "melancholy," as "wretched." She admitted public regret for not honoring Hannah's burial request and chided "those whose conduct had caused her people to desert the homes of their choice and the graves of their proudest chiefs." In the final paragraphs of the column, I.M. clarified her intentions. According to the author's logic, "Columbus was justified in taking advantage of the Arawak's ignorance," but she found "the course pursued by our government towards this rude and unsophisticated people" dishonorable.

The reporter's accusations against the government were largely inspired by current events in which Quakers in particular were taking an interest. Andrew Jackson's implementation of the Indian Removal Act of 1832 was under way, and eighteen hundred Cherokees were encamped on the lower Ohio River when I.M. penned her article. Their forced removal, known as the Trail of Tears, met substantial opposition from many Americans, particularly in the northeastern states. Jeremiah Everts, one of the most effective and persuasive voices challenging Jackson's Indian policy, served as the corresponding secretary of the American Board of Commissioners for Foreign Missions. Ironically, Everts published a series of essays in the *Washington National Intelligencer* in 1829 under the pseudonym William Penn.[8] The essays were reprinted in dozens of papers, inspiring sermons and congressional speeches alike. Despite the highly persuasive moral and historical argument made by "William Penn" in defense of the Cherokees' sovereign rights, land fever and congressional power won the day. Chester County's I.M. pitied the Cherokee condition while admonishing "the cupidity of the white men" in taking lands that did not belong to them. In a final schizophrenic exhortation, the author pitied the Cherokees and the Lenapes, condemned Jackson's greed, but absolved William Penn and his Quaker heirs of any wrongdoing. I.M.'s final determination: Hannah Freeman was the last of her kind.[9]

The next wave of heightened Hannah Freeman nostalgia appeared some thirty years later, spawned by a growing public and academic interest in Indian artifact collections. In the last two decades of the nineteenth century, white Americans were confident that the "Indian problem" was a thing of the past. According to government, military, and scientific assessments, the North American Indians were well on their way to finally "vanishing." The Indian wars were ending; reservations were the final clearinghouse for missionary-led assimilation programs determined to "kill the Indian and save the man."[10] Scholars, artists, and political figures were free to interpret, represent, and study their subjects without interference from a silenced Indian population. Poets, playwrights, and regional historians celebrated America's "noble savages" and selectively harvested their past for details, real or imagined, that would serve to create a believable American identity and history.

Chester County, like many other communities across the United States, enthusiastically joined in the manufacturing of an American past that simultaneously idealized and villainized North American Indians. Relic hunting became a widespread pastime embraced by scholars, antiquarians, collectors, and the general public. Chester County residents shared in this fascination inspired by the pseudo-scientific goals of museums and historical societies and a growing market in American Indian antiquities. Local discoveries of Indian burials, caches of arrowheads, and settlement foundations stimulated an onslaught of interest and questionable expertise. Hannah Freeman, already bestowed with the mantle of "the last of her kind," was frequently referenced in newspaper accounts of the finds, lending spurious authenticity and authority to the information presented.

Offering Hannah as the last survivor confirmed the extinction of the Lenapes and increased the interest in and value of stories and objects connected to Pennsylvania's Indian past. Listed among the "genuine" relics linked to Hannah Freeman was a headband consisting of small and large glass beads woven on hemp cord and leather. The owner, Baldwin Clayton, had acquired the beadwork through a long list of inheritors originating with Sharpless Mercer, "who obtained it from Hannah's effects after her death."[11] Mercer also acquired a set of small silver spoons presumably owned by Hannah. According to Clayton, the spoons were very important to Hannah but she pawned them to Mercer because she was starving. While the spoons never surfaced, the recovery of baskets crafted by Hannah held the local public interest much longer.

Many local antique dealers and antiquarians continue to claim ownership or knowledge of a private collection of these baskets. None of these claims has produced a single item that can be legitimately attributed to Hannah Freeman. Most recently, in 1998, archaeologist Jay Custer investigated a well-known claim regarding two baskets in the possession of the Chester County Historical Society. Custer concluded that while one of the baskets was of a style attributed to southern New England Indians, no clear attributes could confirm or refute the authenticity of the items or definitely link them to Hannah Freeman. Despite his findings, Custer acknowledged that Hannah "has become an icon—a symbol of local Indian heritage important for the region's modern residents," though he dismissed her status "as more myth than reality."[12] By writing off local accounts and regional recollections of Hannah as "mythological," "imaginary," and "fanciful," Custer and other scholars actively contributed to the silencing of Hannah Freeman as a historical actor in Pennsylvania's past. Labeling Hannah Freeman's story as legend and lore undermines the legitimacy and value of her experiences as a Lenape woman in colonial Pennsylvania.

A more fruitful place for a critique of the fanciful, imaginary, and mythological resides within the scores of poems, plays, and images produced to commemorate the Indians in Pennsylvania. Among the more bizarre artifacts held by the Chester County Historical Society is an Indian Hannah cookie carefully wrapped in oiled paper. The date and origin of this "artifact" are unknown, but the cookie's existence means that someone in the community at some point in time manufactured a Hannah Freeman cookie cutter, or at the very least a cutter shaped to represent an Indian woman's head and shoulders. Beginning in 1900 renewed curiosity about Pennsylvania's romanticized Indian past brought new fervor to Hannah Freeman's story. The Lenapes and Hannah Freeman were dramatized and eulogized in family entertainment, public commemoration, and publications. School pageants, claiming historical accuracy, reenacted scenes from the "peaceable kingdom," with local residents playing the parts of "Indian Braves," Indian Squaws," "Indian Maidens," and "Indian Children."[13]

The renewed enthusiasm for Hannah Freeman's story culminated in an organized movement to memorialize her by placing a boulder on the approximate location of her grave. On September 11, 1909, 107 years after Hannah's death, the Chester County Historical Society gathered local dignitaries, historians, and community members to the Chester County Alms House grounds to memorialize Hannah Freeman. There they dedicated a large boulder, retrieved from the Brandywine River, to mark her alleged grave. Sitting under blue skies and the shade of autumn leaves, the audience listened as local historians and dignitaries recounted Chester County's Indian past and in particular Hannah Freeman's story. Eulogizing Hannah, they assured the audience that her last days were happy: "knowing the character of the people of this county . . . we may be sure she received here the same kind and considerate treatment" that the present poorhouse inmates received in the county institution.[11] Dr. George Morris, president of the historical society, reminded the audience that while Chester County had produced many famous men and women, statesman and soldiers, artists and scholars, "we are here to honor the memory of a weak and vanished people." Morris acknowledged the Brandywine land dispute of 1729 and reminded his audience that "the Proprietors acknowledged Lenape claims and for a little longer they lingered here." Morris also pointed out that while the Indians eventually departed, the "land owned by the late Abraham Marshall and . . . the land for a mile on either side of the Brandywine remained for a number of years thus in dispute." Morris's remarks, while acknowledging the illegality of the Lenapes' dispossession, celebrated Hannah Freeman as "the last of her kind." This identity confirmed that the community's unique and persistent interest in her care was motivated by more than historical concerns.

The event allowed members of this predominantly Quaker community to simultaneously allay any guilt regarding their role in Indian land dispossessions and congratulate themselves for their kind and generous treatment of the all but "vanished race." Quaker historian Albert Cook Myers, one of the major organizers of the day's events, took the stage and began the ceremony, offering the gravesite and boulder as tangible proof of Hannah Freeman's status. Professor John R. Hayes, Quaker educator and poet, stepped forward and read a pastoral elegy penned specifically for the event titled "The Indian Grave." Hayes legitimized and gave weight to the ceremony. His great-grandfather, Mordecai Hayes, had signed the "Kindness Extended" and served as treasurer for the group of Quaker men who concerned themselves with Hannah's final care. The author's poetic tribute revealed more about the local community's shared public memory than about Hannah Freeman and the Lenapes. Hayes lamented Hannah as the "last of her race," mourned by "kind Quaker folk." Quakers "who cherished the lone Indian and cared for her" were only trying to ease her suffering. But, according to Hayes, when Hannah died, "so went out a race."[15] The commemorative exercise in 1909 is just one example of how Pennsylvanians struggled to establish a usable Indian past to serve their complex needs. A closer examination of the commemoration and construction of Hannah Freeman as the "last of her kind" and the evidence about her life in Chester County provided by the community presents a stark and often contradictory story. Hannah Freeman personifies the myth of Pennsylvania's benevolent Indian relations in historical memory even though her life as lived is evidence of the myth's falsity.

The chroniclers of Pennsylvania's history, since less than a generation after Hannah's death until the time of Hayes's poem and later, wanted to establish the state's unique role in the master narrative of U.S. history. The absolute "extinction" of Indians within Pennsylvania's borders and accounts of those who vanished into the "west" served the national ideology of manifest destiny. State and regional historians repeatedly cite Hannah's identity as the "last of her kind" as evidence of this certainty.[16] Paradoxically, fixing a unique place in this master narrative for Pennsylvania as the "peaceable kingdom" postulates a benevolent colonial enterprise under which this extinction was somehow more benign than elsewhere. Constructing the history of the benevolent conquest of the Indians in Pennsylvania is, as a result, an occasionally schizophrenic narrative of the state's past.

Hayes's poem reflects the ideological position of many white Americans in the early twentieth century and operates from three assumptions. The first, rooted in the nineteenth-century pseudo-science of social Darwinism, claimed that by 1890 most Americans were satisfied that the last Indian wars had been fought and that the "Indian problem" resided in the domain of missionaries and bureaucrats, not soldiers. According to this thinking, the "Indian" failed to adapt and was therefore unfit for the modern world. This ideology imagines the "Indian" retreating to a metaphorical west, beyond the boundaries of the civilized world. From Hayes's perspective, "territory wrested from [Hannah's] tribe by the intruding English" was a brutal but inevitable consequence: inferior Indians against the superior Anglo-Saxon race. Hayes's poem reflected the popular sentiment legitimized by late nineteenth-century historians and anthropologists who confidently embraced the rhetoric of conquest and racial superiority.[17] The image of the final retreat of the Indian into the setting sun utilized by artists, scholars, and politicians living east of the Mississippi meshed conveniently with the pseudo-scientific theories of racial inferiority and the legitimate science of Darwinian evolution and natural selection. Once the "Indian" had vanished into the west and was doomed to extinction, American image makers could safely romanticize them from a secure temporal and spatial distance.

The second assumption in Hayes's ideological framework draws on the archetypes that emerged from romantic depictions of the historical Indian. The positive archetype granted Indians near sainthood as guardians of the forest and representatives of the utopian natural man. Hayes, in a style and form that imitates nineteenth-century romantic poets, describes the Edenic setting of the Lenapes, where abundant game and fish supported a world of "sylvan loves and war" and the "heroic deeds of deathless chiefs." Primal images abound in Hayes's commemoration as he affectionately imagines the celebration of "strange pagan rites" around "flickering fires." Hannah is likened to the Brandywine River, formerly "wild and wondering" and later old and in "mourning." Hayes furthers the idealized version of the Lenapes as the "noble natives of these hills" by asking Chester County residents to commemorate "in reverence and sorrow" and "pay tribute" to the region's former residents.

J. Carroll Hayes, the poet's brother and a member of the planning committee, made his own artistic contribution to the festivities. He wrote a play that re-created the historic chain of events that culminated in Hannah's death. In order to lend authenticity to his tribute, he turned to the Carlisle Indian School, only a few hours away, as the most likely place to find "suitable" Indians for the celebration. In response to his letter of inquiry, the superintendent of the Carlisle Indian School informed Hayes that the school had four Delaware pupils enrolled, "but they show so small a degree of Indian blood that they would not be typical representatives to assist in your exercises."[18] Apparently, the descendants of the Lenapes held at Carlisle Indian School did not fit the stereotype that both J. Carroll and John R. had come to expect in their reinvention of local Indian history. J. Carroll Hayes needed the "noble red savage" who was both "wild and fierce" and "lofty and proud"—just as his brother had created them. The Delaware students at Carlisle, descendants of the Pennsylvania Lenapes, were not fit to play that part in the ceremonies.

John R. Hayes's poetic elegy to Hannah Freeman does not engage with the negative archetype of the romanticized Indian equally popularized at the beginning of the twentieth century. The demonized Indian makes no appearance in this commemorative event. The bloodthirsty savage had no place in this rendition of public memory, nor did the racialized stereotype of the drunken, lazy Indian nineteenth-century image makers so often employed appear in these memorials. This was the Pennsylvania that Hannah Freeman experienced, according to Hayes. A community of "kind Quaker folk who cherished the lone Indian, cared for her, and made her loneliness less sorrowful." Hostile and resistant Indians or psychically and physically damaged Indians were out of place in a Pennsylvania that was home to the "peaceable kingdom," the Shangri-la of Indian-white relations founded and implemented by William Penn's benevolent and exceptional colonial policies. The savage, bloodthirsty In-

The Betrayal

dian had no purchase on the banks of the Brandywine River, according to its resident historians.

The third and final assumption in this ideological framework is based on the flawed logic of the previous two. Hayes clearly incorporated Hannah Freeman and what she represented in the minds of Chester County residents into his poem. The monolithic and imagined Lenape woman he created was unable to adapt to the modern world brought on by the civilizing forces of European colonization. Hostile resistance was not part of this realization because of the benevolence of Penn's colonial policies. The only alternative available to the Lenapes and other Indians in Pennsylvania, according to this skewed perspective, was to retreat to the western frontier, another imagined landscape. Hannah's refusal to vanish into the west was not seen for what it was—resistance, adaptation, and survivance.[19] Her selective rejection of English culture, her struggle against the forces of colonialism, and her continued occupation of lands that belonged to her family were wrongly interpreted by Hayes and so many others as the desperate, eccentric acts of a lonely old woman deserving of Quaker kindness. She served the chroniclers of Pennsylvania's colonial past as a prized artifact and indisputable evidence that she was "the last of her race . . . lowly and lone." Hayes took this assumption to a new level by enabling Hannah to create an imagined testimony of the changes she had witnessed in her lifetime. Hayes's Hannah Freeman, made familiar to Chester County residents in 1909 through local legend and lore, was an almost animal-like figure, "brooding . . . in gray, autumn twilight by her fire," alone and mourning a past long gone. Her recollections as constructed by Hayes revealed the impact of English invasion: "how the numbers lessened, how the forests fell, and spoiled the hunting, and the fishing failed"; her people "waned" as "farmland after farmland" encroached on the territory her ancestors had governed in "ancient power and wisdom." In the act of assigning the favored memories of the colonizers to the "voice" of Hannah Freeman,

Hayes nearly obliterated from public memory the actual testimony Hannah provided in 1797. The public commemoration in 1909 was meant to mark not only the final resting place of Hannah Freeman, but the final resting place of Pennsylvania's indigenous past.

Epilogue

Nearly one hundred years to the day after the Chester County Historical Society commemorated Hannah Freeman by placing a boulder and plaque on her alleged gravesite, a group of concerned Chester County citizens once again took up the banner to recommemorate the 1909 commemoration. The inscription on the 1909 plaque proclaims:

Here Rests
Indian Hannah
The Last of the Lenni-Lenape
Indians in Chester County
Who Died in 1802

In November 2009 local citizenry dedicated a distinctively larger boulder with the support of the Newlin Township Historical Committee. At first glance it appears that little has changed in this inscription's declaration:

Indian
Hannah
1730–1802
The last
of the tribe of
Lenni-Lenape
in
Chester County

9. Hannah Freeman memorial marker, 2009. (Author's collection)

But a closer examination reveals that the most recent dedication acknowledges the absence of her remains, which in actuality lie unmarked and largely unknown in a field within walking distance of both commemorative boulders. However, the new, more visible marker does little to alter public perceptions that Indian Hannah's remains rest undisturbed beneath the 1909 site. Further, it emphatically declares Hannah Freeman the "last of the tribe of the Lenni-Lenape" despite the fact that the state's official website, hosted by the Pennsylvania Historical and Museum Commission, reports that there are more than fifty thousand Pennsylvanians "with all or some Native American ancestry" and that counted "among that number would be Lenape who considered Hannah a distant relative."[1]

The memorialization of Hannah Freeman that began within one generation of her death continues in modern-day Chester County. "Indian Hannah," a name that is consistently favored over any other, appears in a variety of manifestations from namesake streets to poems read in her honor to historic markers that identify the original location of her "hut." This locally created persona has served the community's needs but betrayed the known realities of her life. From the very beginning in 1824 to the most recent expression, Chester County residents speak of Hannah Freeman with affection, but it is affection inspired largely by pity. There can be no doubt that the story of "Indian Hannah, the last Lenni-Lenape in Chester County" creates a sense of place for many Chester County residents. And the timing of this recommemoration is not without meaning. Unchecked development and suburban sprawl are poised to erase the "unspoiled expanses" that many residents and visitors to the region prize. Until recently a visitor to Chester County could find rolling fields and dense forests, places where one could almost imagine the landscape as Hannah Freeman knew it. Today there are few places remaining along the Brandywine River where one can escape the noise of traffic and local businesses or cast one's gaze up or down the river without seeing power lines or manicured lawns.

Linda Kaat spearheaded the effort to preserve the 1909 marker and create a new site of commemoration. Kaat, a local preservationist and innkeeper, learned that the 1909 site was being used as a dumping ground for a local tree-trimming company. Through her efforts the dumping was stopped and the debris removed. Kaat explained that the community "in death insulted Hannah Freeman's memory by allowing the marker to get forgotten and uncared for and allowing it to become a garbage dump."[2] Kaat's efforts to draw attention to the commemorative boulder launched a grassroots movement to fund a second boulder that would essentially be a larger, more visible replica of the original stone. She explained that many people in the community got involved, but she was especially proud of the participation of the younger residents of Chester County. Local Girl Scout troops raised awareness and collected money, and local business owners placed jars on their store counters to collect the "nickels and pennies" Kaat and her supporters needed to purchase the stone and plaque.

The new commemorative boulder was placed along Route 162 a very short distance from the 1909 site. Kaat explained that the new location was selected because it could be seen from the highway, whereas the older marker was a short distance off the road on a tract of land that until recently had an uncertain future. When Albert Cook Myers, a member of the Chester County Historical Society, led the effort to erect the first monument at the beginning of the twentieth century, the land was owned by Chester County. The site was home to a newer poorhouse that replaced the one Hannah died in and also served as the location of the Chester County Asylum for the Insane. The site selected for the 1909 commemoration is puzzling because it is not the location of the potter's field, nor is it the location of Hannah Freeman's gravesite. The 1909 marker is situated on the original ground of the Chester County Alms House at the top of a hill that at one time presented an open vista of the surrounding countryside and a direct line of sight to the western branch of the Brandywine River where Hannah Freeman spent most of her life. In the correspondence and notes surrounding the original commemoration, Myers and others seemed unaware of or uninterested in the exact location of Hannah's grave or the potter's field; they wanted a symbolic location that served their needs for remembering "Indian Hannah" as the last of her kind.

At the time Myers pursued this early twentieth-century commemoration, there were several rumors and conjectures by those involved about the real location of Hannah's physical remains. Some suggested that her body had been exhumed from the potter's field and buried near the Pierce farm. Others thought she was buried near her birthplace on the Marshall lands near Bennett's Run. One of the most troubling accounts suggested that in the placement of the boulder Hannah's remains were accidentally exhumed. Witnesses claimed that the excavation uncovered a female skeleton with hair intact and remnants of textiles clinging to the bones.[3] Whether there was any truth in the various claims remains inconclusive, but the kind of speculation and avid interest the 1909 commemoration produced reveals the symbolic importance of laying Hannah Freeman and all Lenapes to rest in Chester County. Despite the availability of archival sources that pinpoint the locations of the poorhouse grounds and the site of the adjacent potter's field, the commemoration committee in 1909 moved forward with little regard for the multiple inaccuracies of the marker. Not only was Hanna Freeman not buried under the granite stone atop the hill; she was not the "last Lenni-Lenape" in Chester County.

Despite the best of intentions and the community camaraderie Kaat's 2009 effort produced, the inaccuracies and sentiments remain much the same as they were in 1909. Efforts to resurrect the memory of Hannah Freeman and reacknowledge her place in the community's identity did not arise from a concern for the inaccuracies or misinterpretations of Native American history in the region. They arose from a concern for a monument and a place of enshrinement for a myth that clings tightly to the shores of the Brandywine River and much of Pennsylvania. Hannah Freeman is a highly revered and for many a beloved figure who continues to provide evidence that William Penn's legacy is alive and well in Chester County. The memory of his mythical "peaceable kingdom" and exceptional relationship with the Indians can be found in the embodiment of the fictional "Indian Hannah" that is conjured when needed. The process of marking off historic sites to create shrines and attractions for tourists receives much attention from scholars. Some of this work tries to understand why certain places become sites of commemoration, even to the point of rendering them sacred, when other relatively similar places and sites of significant events or persons are lost and forgotten.[4] Native American history has a unique place in this discussion because until recently the trope of loss, failure, and extinction permeated the historical interpretations of battlefields, monuments, and landscapes, favoring a biased nineteenth-century national narrative. By putting Hannah Freeman's gravesite on display, whether in 1909 or 2009, local residents created a narrative or framework by which those who viewed the site found meaning. In the singular honoring of one Lenape woman, Chester County residents were assured that there were no Indians in Pennsylvania and that the last one had been treated kindly by those who knew her: Indians gone, guilt assuaged. Let the celebrations begin.

In 2009, after a two-year effort by Kaat and the Newlin Township Historical Committee, a group of residents gathered to re-dedicate the now-tended 1909 marker and ceremonially launch the new monument, which Kaat hoped would "send the memory into the next hundred years."[5] On a beautiful November day hauntingly similar to the November day in 1909 when the first commemoration took place, the efforts of "town officials, area residents, artists, academics, Scout groups, and local business-es" culminated in a ceremony that attempted to further legit-imize the nineteenth-century narrative. In a local newspaper account of the ceremony local readers learned that European settlement in the area made it "hard for the Lenape to live in their traditional way, foraging for food . . . and that *all* [Han-nah's] relatives moved away." The reporter makes no mention of the descendants of Lenapes, Nanticokes, Shawnees, and oth-ers who continued to live in New Jersey, Pennsylvania, Mary-land, and Delaware. Nor is there any indication that the cele-bration took place on the anniversary of her incarceration in the poorhouse, not the anniversary of her death: an odd mo-ment in Hannah Freeman's life to commemorate.[6]

The community members gathered in a semicircle around the old monument at the top of the hill. The ground was cleared, weeds pulled, and bluebells, set to bloom each spring, were planted at the old site. One of the members of the historical commission, Linda Sidewater, a native Texan, was asked to do a "smudge ceremony" over the old site. Sidewater, who identifies as Cherokee, performed the ritual to "cleanse and bless" the site, which according to witnesses lent an air of "authenticity" to the event. Various readings and comments were offered at the old monument, including Kaat's reading of the poem Hayes wrote for the 1909 event. Listeners readily accepted Hayes's century-old claim about Hannah Freeman: "Last of her race, she sleeps in this lone grave . . . gently mourned by folk of alien stock, but not alien hearts." The loyal crowd then followed Kaat and the Newlin Township committee members to the bottom of the hill to the site of the new monument along the state highway. This time a group of children were called upon to pull away a "Native American blanket," revealing the monument to the standing crowd—a bigger, better testimony to concerted efforts to preserve a chapter in Chester County's history. The day's events, not unlike those in 1909, ended with food, drink, and festivities at Sidewater's nearby home. According to the reporter, the attendees "left behind a gravesite given back the dignity it deserves and they left behind a marker to help people remember who lies there and what she represented . . . Indian Hannah, the last of her people in Chester County, gently mourned, and long remembered by the people whom came after her."[7]

The reporter's words are severely accurate in a way he probably did not intend. The gravesite, the marker, and what they represent are most significant to those involved in the rededication of the site, not Hannah Freeman and certainly not the Lenapes. But the tragedy here and the real sense of loss that remains unappeased are the myths and misinterpretations recently given new life. Neither Kaat nor any members of the committee made any effort to contact the Delaware and Lenape communities in New Jersey, Oklahoma, or Ontario, Canada. When asked if any effort was made to connect with the living descendants of the Lenapes from southeastern Pennsylvania so they might participate in the rededication, Sidewater responded that Hannah "really was the last of her kind." She said there "are no more Delawares or Lenapes." When reminded of the communities beyond historic Pennsylvania, she responded doubtfully, "Oh, them . . ."[8]

Linda Poolaw, a member of the Delaware Nation in Anadarko, Oklahoma, would have been very happy to participate in remembering one of the grandmothers of the Lenapes. Poolaw, former secretary of the Delaware Nation, educator, writer, and perhaps most well known as a storyteller, has a wealth of knowledge about her people and their history, especially as it pertains to women. In 2010 I had the opportunity to share Hannah Freeman's story with Poolaw and other Native women and men attending a Delaware Symposium held at her nation's headquarters in western Oklahoma. Poolaw identified with Hannah Freeman in an unexpected way. "When you are the oldest," she said, referring to herself, "there is no one left to ask questions of. What Hannah knew a long time ago is part of what I know today."[9] Linda Poolaw, like many of the descendants of Pennsylvania's first people, whether living in Oklahoma, Canada, New Jersey, or even Pennsylvania, continue to honor the legacy of their ancestors in many ways. Those who commemorate Hannah Freeman as the "last Lenape" would do well to remember this.

The efforts to memorialize Hannah Freeman were sincere both in 1909 and 2009, but they were misguided. So many sites of memory and commemoration are under scrutiny for misleading modern audiences or for omitting information they have the right to know. The public sites where observers learn Native American history are especially suspect in this regard because most were a product of less enlightened periods of our nation's history. But those who make the effort to rectify this inequity, whether by erecting new places of commemoration or by revisiting inaccurate or neglected public monuments, markers, and landscapes in order to make changes that honor all our pasts, must be careful to do good research and involve the communities whose stories they seek to interpret.

I did not learn about Hannah Freeman from a roadside marker or a misplaced boulder. Hannah Freeman entered my life through the usual route for a historian, a document from an archive. Fortunately for me, that first encounter emanated from her voice, in the testimony she gave to Moses Marshall in 1797. However, every research trip I have made to Chester County over the years has included a visit to the 1909 marker to pay my respects, even though I know she is not there. It was on just such a trip that I encountered the 2009 marker. But more important than my visits to a commemorative boulder are the walks I take along the Brandywine River, remembering and honoring the perseverance and survivance of Hannah Freeman, Turtle Island's daughter.

The Examination of Indian Hannah
alias Hannah Freeman

July 28, 1797
Moses Marshall, Overseer of the Poor

The Examination of Indian Hannah, alias, Hannah Freeman
Who saith she was born in a Cabin on William Webb's Place in
the Township of Kennett about the year 1730 or 31. The family
consisting of her Grandmother Jane Aunts Betty & Nanny, her
Father and Mother used to live in their Cabin at Webb's place
in the Winter and in the Summer moved to Newlin to Plant
Corn. She was born in the month of March. The Family continued living in Kennett & Newlin alternatively for several years after her birth as She has two brothers born there younger than
herself. The Country becoming more settled the Indians were
not allowed to Plant Corn any longer her father went to Shamokin and never returned, the rest of the Family moved to Centre in Christianna, New Castle County and lived in a Cabin on
Swithin Chandler's place they continued living in their Cabins
sometimes in Kennett and sometimes at Centre till the Indians were killed at Lancaster soon after which they being afraid,
moved over the Delaware to N. Jersey and lived with the Jersey Indians for about Seven Years after which her Granny Jane,
Aunt Betty and Nanny her mother & Self came back and lived
in Cabins sometimes at Kennett at Centre, at Brinton's place
and Chester Creek occasionally as best suited. This mode of
living was continued till the family decreased her Granny died
above Schuylkill her Aunt Betty at Middletown, and her Moth-

er at Centre, her mother died about the time Thomas Buffington's first wife died. Soon after her Mothers death which was in the Fall she went to live with her Aunt Nanny at Concord & staid with her all winter she then returned to Centre and lived a little while at Swithin Chandler's (maybe two months) then went to White Tho Chandler's in N. Castle County where she lived about two years worked at Sewing &c and received 3/6 per week wages, from there to Black Tho Chandler's where she staid about three Years, Sewing &c and rec'd wages or Sheets for her work. She then went again to Swithin Chandler's for a few weeks & rec'd 3/6 per week wages. She worked a few weeks in some other places at Gideon Gilpin's &c. then went to her Aunt Nanny at Concord but having almost forgot to talk Indian and not liking their manner of living so well as white peoples she came to Kennett & lived at Wm Webbs worked for her board sometime but got no money except for baskets, besoms &c She lived at Sam Levis three years that is made her home & worked sometimes for her board but rec'd nowages, but made baskets &c. Since this time she has been moving about from place to place making baskets &c and staying longest where best used but never was hired or rec'd wages except for baskets &c but at Centre amongst the Chandlers.

Kindness Extended

Joseph Barnard, 3ʀᴅ Month, 1798

Hannah Freeman Commonly Called Indian Hannah an ancient Woman of the Delaware Tribe and the only Person of that Description left amongst us being afflicted with Rheumatism and unable to support herself accustomed to Travel from house to House which is sometimes attended with great difficulty and Inconvenience it is thought her situation Claims the Sympathy of the humane in order that she may be more Regularly and Permanently Provided for in a manner suited to her Usual way of living. Therefore Be it Remembered that We the Subscribers do severally agree to Contribute towards her maintenance (if Providence Should favour us with ability) Yearly and every Year during her Natural Life in Money or otherwise agreeable to what we Subscribe Subject to the Disposal of two Guardians or Trustees and a Treasurer Annually appointed at a Meeting of the Subscribers on the first 2nd day in the Eleventh Month at one O'Clock on said day at the house of Richard Barnard at which time Said Trustees are to Produce full accounts of what they have Received and expended on the occation which Service is submitted to the care of Mordicai Hayes and Jacob Peirce for the Present Year and Joseph Barnard Named for Treasurer who is not to pay anyting out of the Stock without Wrtin Orders from one of the Trustees, And after the Decease her funeral Expenses being Discharged if there Should be an overplus the Trustees and Treasurer are, to Return it to the subscribers in Proportion to what they have advanced.

Subscribers to keep her and the times per year

	Weeks	Days
Richard Barnard	2	
Joseph Barnard	1	
Samuel Marshall	1	2
William Allen	2	
Rich'd Bernard Jnr.	1	
Isaac Baily Ju.	1	
William Smith	1	2
Caleb Harlan	1	
Mordecai Hayes	1	2
Jess Taylor	1	
James Pyle	1	3
Jacob Peirce	1	0
Solomon Mercer	1	0

Subscribers to pay money

	£	s	d
Richard Jones Jr		7	6
Tho Lugar		2	6
Joshua Buffington		7	6
George Speakman		5	7½
James Smith		7	6
Enoch Taylor		7	6
Charles Wilson		7	6
Wm Butler		7	6
James Steen		3	9
Philip Wand		3	9
William Hall		3	9
Wm Wickersham		3	9
Caleb Wickersham		2	6
Charles Wilson Jr.		3	9
Stephen Harlen		3	9
James Embree		3	2

	£	s	d
Isaac Bayley		7	6
Samuel Pennock		3	9

At a meeting of a Number of the Subscribers held at Richard Barnards the 4th day of the 11th Month of 1799 Mordicai Hayes and Jacob Peirce are appointed Trustees in the case of Indian Hannah agreeable to the writtin Article Joseph Barnard is Continued our Treasurer and Richard Barnard and Caleb Harlen are appointed to assist them. Signed on behalf and by Direction of said Meeting By Joseph Barnard

The under Named Persons have Paid agreeable to their subscription on Indian Hannah's Account for the Year 1798.

	£	s	d
Richard Jones		7	6
Thomas Lugar		2	6
Isaac Bayley		7	6

Notes

Introduction

1. Becker, "Hannah Freeman," 249.

2. *Survivance* is a term coined by Anishanaabe critic and writer Gerald Vizenor to counter the colonialist language of absence, tragedy, and powerlessness usually engendered in Native American scholarship. See *Manifest Manners*, vii, 4–44.

3. For more on the historiography of Native American history in Pennsylvania, see Richter, "The Indian in Pennsylvania."

4. For the Walking Purchase Treaty, see Jennings, "The Scandalous Indian Policy of William Penn's Sons"; Harper, *Promised Land*, 28–45. For the Paxton Massacre, see Hindle, "The March of the Paxton Boys"; Martin, "The Return of the Paxton Boys."

5. O'Brien, *Dispossession by Degrees*.

6. Murphy, "Autonomy and Economic Roles of Indian Women"; Braund, "Guardians of Tradition and Handmaids to Change."

1. The Examination of Hannah Freeman

1. Indians, Albert Cook Myers Collection (hereafter cited as ACMC), Chester County Historical Society, West Chester PA (hereafter cited as CCHS).

2. Indians, ACMC.

3. Nash, *First City*, 1–14.

4. On the interchangeability of Lenape-Delaware: Lenape is the name the people call themselves. Delaware is a product of the colonial encounter. Delaware is more often used after the mid-eighteenth century. Today the people use both names.

5. *Population Schedules of the First Census of the United States, 1790*.

6. Thomas Jefferson to George Rogers Clark, December 25, 1780, *Papers of Thomas Jefferson*, 237–38. On the use of "last of their kind," see O'Brien, *Firsting and Lasting*, 116–18.

7. Penn, "A Further Account of the Province of Pennsylvania"; Penn, "To the Kings of the Indians."

8. Spady, "Colonialism and the Discursive Antecedents of Penn's Treaty with the Indians"; "Complaint of the Brandywine Indians."

9. Grumet, "Sunsquaws, Shamans, and Tradeswomen"; Schoenenberger, *Lenape Women, Matriliny, and the Colonial Encounter*, 141–44.

10. Barnard diary, CCHS; Futhey and Cope, *History of Chester County*, 1428–31.

11. Hazard, *Pennsylvania Archives*, 239–40.

12. Rothenberg, "Friends Like These," 122–30.

13. Marshall, "Examination of Indian Hannah," CCHS.

14. "Memorial to Humphry and Moses Marshall"; Futhey and Cope, *History of Chester County*, 652.

15. Futhey and Cope, *History of Chester County*, 191–92.

16. Wawasan is a locally recognized but linguistically unverified "Indian name" for the Brandywine River. Mowday, *Along the Brandywine River*, 47.

17. Saffron, "Wrecking Ball Threatens West Chester Boom."

18. Futhey and Cope, *History of Chester County*, 215.

19. "West Chester"; *Design Guidelines for the West Chester Historic District*.

20. Marshall, "Examination of Indian Hannah," CCHS.

21. "An Act for the Relief of the Poor."

22. Barnard diary, CCHS.

23. Barnard, "Kindness Extended," CCHS.

24. Winter, newspaper clipping, Indian File, CCHS.

25. Simler, "She Came to Work," 429–32.

26. Chester County Directors of the Poor, "Minutes," November 5, 1798, through November 7, 1803, Chester County Archives, West Chester PA (hereafter cited as CCA).

27. Chester County Directors of the Poor, "Minutes," November 21, 1798, March 1, 1799, CCA.

28. Borque, "The Peculiar Characteristic of Christian Communities," 61–63; Chester County Directors of the Poor, "Minutes," November 1798, CCA.

29. Court of Private Sessions, CCA, 147–50; Chester County Poorhouse Admissions and Discharges, CCA.

2. All Our Grandmothers

1. Speck and Witapanóxwe, *A Study of the Delaware Indian Big House Ceremony*, 49; Wassenarer, "Historisch Verhael," 68–69.

2. "The Charter of Pennsylvania."

3. "Petition to Charles II."

4. "John Moll's Account of the Surrender of the Three Lower Counties to William Penn"; "An Abstract of a Letter to Philip Ford from William Penn."

5. E. Willard Miller, *A Geography of Pennsylvania*, 2.

6. Donck, *A Description of New Netherland*, 29–31; Juet, "The Third Voyage of Master Henry Hudson"; de Laet, "New World," 53.

7. de Laet, "New World," 52–54; Lindeström, *Geographia Americae*, 221–35; Donck, *A Description of New Netherland*, 73–94.

8. Gustavas Hesselius, "Portrait of Lapowinsa."

9. Goddard, "Delaware."

10. Gabriel Thomas, "An Historical and Geographical Account of Pensilvania and of West-New-Jersey," 344.

11. Becker, "Lenape Maize Sales to the Swedish Colonists," 122–23.

12. Kraft, "Indian Prehistory of New Jersey," 33–34.

13. Anthony F. C. Wallace, "Women, Land and Society," 16; Newcomb, *The Culture and Acculturation of the Delaware Indians,* 13–20.

14. Kraft, *The Lenape,* 143–46, 201–10.

15. Penn, "To the Inhabitants of Pennsylvania."

16. Penn, "Some Account of the Province of Pennsylvania."

17. Penn, "Conditions or Concessions to the First Purchasers."

18. Goddard, "Delaware."

19. Schutt, *Peoples of the River Valleys,* 98–101.

20. Dunn and Dunn, *The Papers of William Penn,* 242–43.

21. Spady, "Colonialism and the Discursive Antecedents of Penn's Treaty with the Indians," 38–39.

22. Penn, "To the Kings of the Indians," 88.

23. Penn, "Additional Instructions to William Markham."

24. "Deed from the Delaware Indians."

25. Lemon, *The Best Poor Man's Country,* 4–5, 23.

26. Penn, "Letter to the Free Society of Traders."

27. Penn, "Letter to the Free Society of Traders."

28. Penn, "Letter to the Free Society of Traders."

29. Penn-Physick Papers, Historical Society of Pennsylvania (hereafter HSP).

30. Minutes of the Board of Property.

31. Rigel, "Framing the Fabric," 557.

32. Gordon, *The History of Pennsylvania,* 75–76.

33. Jennings, "Brother Miquon," 206, 208–10.

34. "Votes of the Assembly," *Pennsylvania Archives,* ser. 8, vol. 2, 1757–59.

35. Egle, *Pennsylvania Archives,* 216–67.

36. George Harlan, Warrant, Records of the Land Office, Register of Old Rights, 1682–1733, Harrisburg PA.

37. Marshall, "Examination of Indian Hannah," CCHS.

38. "Votes of the Assembly," *Pennsylvania Archives,* ser. 8, vol. 2, 1757–59.

39. James Logan to William Penn, September 15, 1706, 167.

40. Andreas Hesselius and Johnson, *The Journal of Andreas Hesselius.*

41. Futhey and Cope, *History of Chester County,* 190–92.

42. "Votes of the Assembly," *Pennsylvania Archives,* ser. 8, vol. 2, 1757–59.

43. Weslager, *The Delaware,* 183.

44. Statements by Nathaniel Newlin and the Commissioner of Property on the Brandywine Indians' Complaint, 1726, Logan Family Papers, Indian Affairs, HSP.

45. Statements by Nathaniel Newlin and the Commissioner of Property

on the Brandywine Indians' Complaint, 1726, Logan Family Papers, Indian Affairs, HSP.

46. "Votes of the Assembly," *Pennsylvania Archives*, ser. 8, vol. 2, 1757–59.

47. Schutt. *Peoples of the River Valleys*, 74–89.

48. Gist, *Christopher Gist's Journals*, 142–43; Kenny, "Journal of James Kenny."

3. The Peaceable Kingdom

1. Indians, ACMC, CCHS; Futhey and Cope, *History of Chester County*, 162, 625.

2. Marsh, "Creating Delaware Homelands in the Ohio Country."

3. Indians, ACMC, CCHS.

4. Indian Hannah File, Newspaper Clippings, CCHS.

5. Weslager, "Delaware Indian Name Giving and Modern Practice"; Dean, "Some of the Ways of the Delaware Indian Women."

6. Holm, *A Short Description of the Province of New Sweden*, 126–28; Nash, *Forging Freedom*, 80, 85.

7. Heckewelder, *History, Manner and Customs of the Indian Nations*, 440; James A. Rementer, personal communication, 2008.

8. Merritt, *At the Crossroads*, 58.

9. Marshall, "Examination of Indian Hannah," CCHS.

10. Fur, *A Nation of Women*, 16–36.

11. Schoenenberger, *Lenape Women, Matriliny, and the Colonial Encounter*, 115–16; Anthony F. C. Wallace, "Political Organization and Land Tenure among the Northeastern Indians," 311–12.

12. Smith, "A Map of Virginia"; Williams, *A Key Into the Language of North America*, 98–102.

13. Swann, *Coming to Light*, 491.

14. Heckewelder, *History, Manner and Customs of the Indian Nations*, 47–70.

15. Tooker, *Native North American Spirituality of the Eastern Woodlands*, 104–9.

16. Bierhorst, *Mythology of the Lenape*, 5–12; Brinton, *The Lenape and Their Legends*.

17. Harrington, "Some Customs of the Delaware Indians," 54–55.

18. Brock, *The Quaker Peace Testimony*.

19. Jay Miller, "Old Religion among the Delawares," 115–16.

20. Marshall, "Examination of Indian Hannah," CCHS.

21. Indians, ACMC, CCHS.

22. Holm, *A Short Description of the Province of New Sweden*, 47, 130–31; Lindeström, *Geographia Americae*, 223–25.

23. Hood, "The Material World of Cloth."

24. Simler, "She Came to Work"; Jensen, *Loosening the Bonds*, 36–51.

25. Marshall, "Examination of Indian Hannah," CCHS.

26. Ulrich, "Wheels, Looms, and the Gender Division of Labor in Eighteenth Century New England."

27. Tantaquidgeon, *Folk Medicine of the Delaware*, 5–10; Dean, "Remembrances of the Big House Church," 47.

28. Heckewelder, *History, Manners, and Customs of the Indian Nations*, 228–32.

29. Tantaquidgeon, *Folk Medicine of the Delaware*, 5–27.

30. Indians, ACMC, CCHS.

31. Darlington, *Memorials of John Bartram and Humphry Marshall*.

32. Futhey and Cope, *History of Chester County*, 225, 315.

33. Marietta and Rowe, *Troubled Experiment*, 71–72, 107.

34. Penn, "To the Kings of the Indians," 88.

35. Wokeck, *Trade in Strangers*, 5, 38.

36. Schwartz, *"A Mixed Multitude,"* 81–119.

37. Simler and Clemens, "The Best Poor Man's Country in 1783," 245.

38. Marietta and Rowe, *Troubled Experiment*, 175; Block, *Rape and Sexual Power in Early America*, 53–87.

39. Quarter Sessions Indictments, CCA.

40. Quarter Sessions Indictments, CCA.

41. Mitchell and Flanders, *The Statues at Large of Pennsylvania*.

42. Marietta and Rowe, *Troubled Experiment*, 155–56.

4. Lenapehoking Lost

1. Marshall, "Examination of Indian Hannah," CCHS.

2. Merritt, *At the Crossroads*, 3–5 (on crossroads as metaphor), 33–36 (on Shamokin).

3. Paul A. W. Wallace, *Indian Paths of Pennsylvania*, 64–75.

4. Bartram, *Observations*, 14–15.

5. Merrell, "Shamokin," 22.

6. Anthony F. C. Wallace, "Women, Land and Society," 6–14.

7. Marshall, "Examination of Indian Hannah," CCHS. "Hundreds" are subdivision of counties used in colonial Delaware. They are equivalent to townships in other colonies.

8. Watson, *Annals of Philadelphia and Pennsylvania in the Olden Time*, 70.

9. Advertisement, Guarantee Trust and Safe Deposit Company, *Philadelphia Evening Public Ledger*, October 29, 1919.

10. Chester County Surveys, 1701–1740, HSP; Chester County Warrants, 1682–1748, HSP; New Castle County, Del., Warrants and Surveys, 1679–1740, HSP; Jacob and Isaac Taylor Papers, 1672–1775, HSP.

11. Scharfe, *The History of Delaware*, 920–21.

12. Jones, *The Later Periods of Quakerism*, 407; Tolles, *Meeting House and Counting House*, 3–29.

13. Tetamie, "An Account of the Walking Purchase"; Jennings, "The Scandalous Indian Policy of William Penn's Sons."

14. Johnson, *The Papers of Sir William Johnson*, 788; Jennings, *The Ambiguous Iroquois Empire*, chapters 16–17; Harper, *Promised Land*.

15. Newman, "'Light might possibly be requisite,'" 340.

16. *Delaware Nation v. Pennsylvania*, U.S. Dist. 166 (2004); *Delaware Nation v. Pennsylvania*, 446 F.3d 410, 3d Cir. (2006).

17. Miscellaneous Papers of the Pre-separation Meeting, Epistles, Records of the Philadelphia Yearly Meeting, Swarthmore College Library, Swarthmore PA.

18. Moore, *Friends in the Delaware Valley*, 27.

19. James Logan to Conrad Weiser, July 11, 1742, Peters Papers, 1697–1845, HSP.

20. Bond, "The Captivity of Charles Stuart," 63.

21. Merritt, *At the Crossroads*, 176–80.

22. Berkeley and Berkeley, *The Correspondence of John Bartram*, 400.

23. Barnard, "Kindness Extended," CCHS.

24. "Votes of the Assembly," *Pennsylvania Archives*, ser. 8, vol. 2, 4245–50; "Votes of the Assembly," *Pennsylvania Archives*, ser. 8, vol. 6, 4664.

25. Records of the Proprietary Government, Official Correspondence, Peters to Proprietors, July 5, 1749; Peters, Report to the Assembly, 445, 448.

26. *Minutes of the Provincial Council of Pennsylvania*, 5:443, 448.

27. Papers of the Friendly Association for Regaining and Preserving Peace with the Indians by Pacific Measures, Quaker Collection, Haverford College, 1:103.

28. Marshall, "Examination of Indian Hannah," CCHS.

29. Dowd, *A Spirited Resistance*, 32–33.

30. Dowd, *War under Heaven*.

31. Franklin, "A Narrative of the Late Massacres, in Lancaster County, of a Number of Indians, Friends of this Province, by Persons Unknown"; "Smith and Gibson, "A Declaration and Remonstrance of the Distressed and Bleeding Frontier Inhabitants of the Province of Pennsylvania," 72, 107.

32. Marshall, "Examination of Indian Hannah," CCHS.

5. Kindness Extended

1. Brinton, *The Lenapes and Their Legends*, 130–35, 137.

2. Heckewelder, *History, Manners and Customs of the Indian Nations*, 47–53.

3. Journal of the Governor and Council, 1748–1755, in Ricord, *Documents relating to the Colonial History of New Jersey*, 572–73.

4. Journal of the Governor and Council, 1748–1755, in Ricord, *Documents relating to the Colonial History of New Jersey*, 572–73.

5. Nelson, *Documents relating to the Colonial History of the State of New Jersey*, 42–44; Ricord, *Documents relating to the Colonial History of New Jersey*, 38–40.

6. Franklin, "A Narrative of the Late Massacres, in Lancaster County, of a Number of Indians, Friends of this Province, by Persons Unknown," 53–60; Moravian Indian Diaries.

7. Ricord, *Documents relating to the Colonial History of New Jersey*, 362–63; Stewart, *Notes on Old Gloucester County*, 262–63.

8. Marshall, "Examination of Indian Hannah," CCHS.

9. Indians, ACMC, CCHS.

10. "Records of the Kennett Monthly Meeting," Centre Preparative Meeting, Friends Historical Library, Swarthmore College, Swarthmore PA.

11. Lyons, *X-Marks*, 4–13, 37–38.

12. Marshall, "Examination of Indian Hannah," CCHS.

13. Indians, ACMC, CCHS.

14. Indians, ACMC, CCHS; Hayes, "Little Journeys in Chester County."

15. Simler, "She Came to Work," 442–45.

16. Indians, ACMC, CCHS; *West Chester Village Record*, June 23, 1824.

17. Glatthaar and Martin, *Forgotten Allies*, 149.

18. Futhey, "An Address on the Paoli Massacre"; Sullivan, "Before and After the Battle of Brandywine," 412–13.

19. Marshall, "Examination of Indian Hannah," CCHS.

20. "Joseph Townsend's Account of the Battle of Brandywine," in Futhey and Cope, *History of Chester County*, 236–45.

21. U.S. Constitution, art. I, sec. 8.

22. Brooks, *The Common Pot*, 106–62.

23. Indians, ACMC, CCHS.

24. Becker, "Hannah Freeman," 265–66.

25. Indians, ACMC, CCHS.

26. "For the Village Record"; I.M., "Reminiscences for the Register."

27. Harrington, *Religion and Ceremonies of the Lenape*, 29–30.

28. Indians, ACMC, CCHS; Smith, *The History of Delaware County*, 400.

29. Dean, "Touching Leaves Woman Recalls Past."

30. Dean, "Touching Leaves Woman Recalls Past."

31. "Delaware Indian Reminiscences"; James A. Rementer, personal communication, 2008.

32. Indians, ACMC, CCHS.

33. Bromberg and Shephard, "The Quaker Burial Ground in Alexandria, Virginia," 61–63.

34. "Lenape Funeral Customs"; Heckewelder, *History, Manners and Customs of the Indian Nations*, 268–76.

35. Marshall, "Examination of Indian Hannah," CCHS.

36. Barnard, "Kindness Extended," CCHS.

37. Jackson, "Halliday Jackson's Journal to the Seneca Indians, 1798–1800."

38. Marshall, "Examination of Indian Hannah," CCHS.

39. Barnard, "Kindness Extended," CCHS.

6. The Betrayal

1. Minutes of the Directors of the Poor, CCA.

2. Chester County Poorhouse Admissions and Discharges, book 1, CCA.

3. Chester County Poorhouse Admissions and Discharges, book 1, CCA.

4. Indians, ACMC, CCHS.

5. Newman, "'Light might possibly be requisite,'" 322–23, 332–33.

6. E., "Poem," *West Chester Village Record,* June 23, 1824, CCHS.

7. I.M., "Reminiscences for the Register."

8. Prucha, *"William Penn" Essays.*

9. I.M., "Reminiscences for the Register."

10. Pratt, *Proceedings of the National Conference of Charities and Correction,* 45.

11. Untitled newspaper column, June 21, 1894, Indian Hannah File, CCHS.

12. Custer, "Hannah Freeman's Baskets."

13. Indian Hannah File, CCHS.

14. "In Memory of Indian Hannah."

15. "In Memory of Indian Hannah." Subsequent quotations from Hayes's poem are drawn from this source.

16. The earliest regional history that identifies Hannah Freeman as the "last of her race" can be found in Watson, *Annals of Philadelphia and Pennsylvania in the Olden Time,* 70, 447.

17. Thomas, *Skull Wars,* 51–67.

18. Indians, ACMC, CCHS.

19. Vizenor, *Manifest Manners,* vii.

Epilogue

1. "Indian Hannah Historical Marker."

2. Linda Kaat, telephone interview with author, August 22, 2011.

3. Indians, ACMC, CCHS.

4. Forristal and Marsh, "Maccannell's Site Sacralization Theory."

5. Linda Kaat, telephone interview with author, August 22, 2001.

6. Freeman, "Indian Hannah Grave Site Rededicated."

7. Freeman, "Indian Hannah Grave Site Rededicated."

8. Linda Sidewater, telephone interview with author, August 22, 2011.

9. Linda Poolaw, interview with author, Delaware Nation, Anadarko OK, November 2010.

Bibliography

Primary Sources

"An Abstract of a Letter to Philip Ford from William Penn." In *William Penn and the Founding of America: A Documentary History*, edited by Jean Soderlund, 188. Philadelphia: University of Pennsylvania Press, 1983.

"An Act for the Relief of the Poor." In *The Statutes at Large of Pennsylvania from 1682–1801*, 2:251–54. Harrisburg: Clarence M. Busch, 1896.

Advertisement, Guarantee Trust and Safe Deposit Company. *Philadelphia Evening Public Ledger*, October 29, 1919.

Barnard, Richard. Diary, 1774–1792. Chester County Historical Society, West Chester PA.

———. "Kindness Extended," March 1798. Chester County Historical Society, West Chester PA.

Bartram, John. *Observations on the Inhabitants, Climate, Soil, Rivers, Productions, Animals and Other Matters of Worthy Notice.* London: J. Whiston and B. White, 1751.

Berkeley, Edmund, and Dorothy Smith Berkeley. *The Correspondence of John Bartram, 1734–1777.* Miami: University of Florida Press, 1992.

Bond, Beverly W., Jr. "The Captivity of Charles Stuart, 1755–57." *Mississippi Historical Review* 13 (June 1926): 58–81.

"The Charter of Pennsylvania," March 4, 1681. In *William Penn and the Founding of Pennsylvania: A Documentary History*, edited by Jean Soderlund, 41–49. Philadelphia: University of Pennsylvania Press, 1983.

Chester County Directors of the Poor. "Minutes," November 5, 1798, through November 7, 1803. Chester County Archives, West Chester PA.

Chester County Poorhouse Admissions and Discharges, 1800–1858. Chester County Archives, West Chester PA.

Chester County Surveys, 1701–1740. Historical Society of Pennsylvania, Philadelphia.

Chester County Warrants, 1682–1748. Historical Society of Pennsylvania, Philadelphia.

Clippings Files. Chester County Historical Society, West Chester PA.

"Complaint of the Brandywine Indians." In *Pennsylvania Archives*, ser. 8, vol. 2, edited by Gertrude MacKinney, 1701–5. Harrisburg, 1931–35.

Court of Private Sessions, 1766–1826. Chester County Archives, West Chester PA.

Darlington, Edward. *Memorials of John Bartram and Humphry Marshall, with Notices of Botanical Contemporaries*. Philadelphia: Lindsay Blakiston, 1849.

Dean, Nora Thompson. "Delaware Indian Reminiscences." *Bulletin of the Archaeological Society of New Jersey* 35 (1978): 1–17.

———. "Lenape Funeral Customs." In *The Lenape Indian: A Symposium*, edited by Herbert C. Kraft, 63–70. South Orange NJ: Archaeological Research Center, Seton Hall University, 1984.

———. "Remembrances of the Big House Church." In *The Lenape Indian: A Symposium*, edited by Herbert C. Kraft, 41–49. South Orange NJ: Archaeological Research Center, 1984.

———. "Some of the Ways of the Delaware Indian Women," 1983. Unpublished manuscript. Dewey OK.

———. "Touching Leaves Woman Recalls Past." *Dewey Herald Record*, August 1983.

"Deed from the Delaware Indians." In *William Penn and the Founding of Pennsylvania: A Documentary History*, edited by Jean Soderlund, 156–58. Philadelphia: University of Pennsylvania Press, 1983.

de Laet, Johannes. "New World." In *Narratives of New Netherland, 1609–1664*, edited by J. Franklin Jameson. New York: Charles Scribner's Sons, 1909.

Delaware Nation v. Pennsylvania. U.S. Dist. 166 (2004).

Delaware Nation v. Pennsylvania. 446 F.3d 410, 3d Cir. (2006).

Design Guidelines for the West Chester Historic District. West Chester: West Chester Historical and Architectural Review Board, July 2002.

Donck, Adriaen van der. *A Description of New Netherland*. Edited by Charles T. Gehring and William A. Starna. Lincoln: University of Nebraska Press, 2008.

Dunn, Mary Maples, and Richard S. Dunn, eds. *The Papers of William Penn: 1680–84*. Vol. 2. Philadelphia: University of Pennsylvania Press, 1981.

E. "Poem." *West Chester Village Record*, June 23, 1824. Chester County Historical Society, West Chester PA.

Egle, William H., ed. *Pennsylvania Archives*. Ser. 2, vol. 19. Harrisburg: State Printer, 1890.

"For the Village Record." *West Chester Village Record*, June 23, 1824. Chester County Historical Society, West Chester PA.

Franklin, Benjamin. "A Narrative of the Late Massacres, in Lancaster County, of a Number of Indians, Friends of This Province, by Persons Unknown." In *The Paxton Papers*, edited by John R. Dunbar, 55–75. The Hague: Martinus Nijhoff, 1957.

———. *The Papers of Benjamin Franklin.* Vol. 11. Edited by Leonard Larabee. New Haven: Yale University Press, 1967.

Freeman, Matt. "Indian Hannah Grave Site Rededicated." *West Chester Daily Local News,* November 28, 2009.

Gist, Christopher. *Christopher Gist's Journals.* Edited by William Darlington. Pittsburgh: J. R. Weldin, 1893.

Harlan, George. Warrant, Records of the Land Office, Register of Old Rights, 1682–1733. Pennsylvania State Archives, Harrisburg PA.

Hayes, J. Carroll. "Little Journeys in Chester County," n.d. Indian File, Albert Cook Myers Collection, Chester County Historical Society, West Chester PA.

Hazard, Samuel, ed. *Pennsylvania Archives.* Ser. 1, vol. 1. Philadelphia: Joseph Severns, 1852.

Heckewelder, John. *History, Manner and Customs of the Indian Nations Who Once Inhabited Pennsylvania and the Neighboring States.* 1819. Reprint, New York: Arno, 1971.

Hesselius, Andreas, and Amandus Johnson. *The Journal of Andreas Hesselius, 1711–1724.* Philadelphia: Joseph Severns, 1947.

Hesselius, Gustavas. "Portrait of Lapowinsa," 1735. Historical Society of Pennsylvania Collection, Atwater Kent Museum, Philadelphia.

Holm, Thomas Campanius. *A Short Description of the Province of New Sweden: Now Called by the English, Pennsylvania, in America.* Translated by Peter S. Du Ponceau. Philadelphia, 1834.

I.M. "Reminiscences for the Register." *West Chester Register and Examination,* February 26, 1839.

Indian File. Albert Cook Myers Collection, Chester County Historical Society, West Chester PA.

Indian Hannah File. Newspaper Clippings. Albert Cook Myers Collection, Chester County Historical Society, West Chester PA.

"Indian Hannah Historical Marker." *Stories of Pennsylvania's Past and Present.* Pennsylvania Historical and Museum Commission. http://explorepahistory.com/hmarker.php?markerId=1-A-226 (accessed April 13, 2013).

Indians. Albert Cook Myers Collection, Chester County Historical Society, West Chester PA.

"In Memory of Indian Hannah." *West Chester Daily Local News,* September 13, 1909. Indians. Albert Cook Myers Collection, Chester County Historical Society, West Chester PA.

Jackson, Halliday. "Halliday Jackson's Journal to the Seneca Indians, 1798–1800." Edited by Anthony F. C. Wallace. *Pennsylvania History* 19, no. 2 (1952): 117–44.

Jefferson, Thomas. *The Papers of Thomas Jefferson.* Vol. 4. Edited by Julian P. Boyd. Princeton: Princeton University Press, 1950.

"John Moll's Account of the Surrender of the Three Lower Counties to William Penn," 1682. In *Papers of William Penn*, edited by Mary Maples Dunn and Richard S. Dunn, 2:304–8. Philadelphia: University of Pennsylvania Press, 1986.

Johnson, William. *The Papers of Sir William Johnson*. Vol. 3. Edited by J. Sullivan. Albany: State University of New York, 1921.

Juet, Robert. "The Third Voyage of Master Henry Hudson." In *Narratives of New Netherland, 1609–1664*, edited by J. Franklin Jameson, 18–37. New York: Charles Scribner's Sons, 1909.

Kenny, James. "Journal of James Kenny, 1761–1763." *Pennsylvania Magazine of History and Biography* 32, no. 1 (1913): 1–47.

Lindeström, Peter. *Geographia Americae, with an Account of the Delaware Indians*. Translated by Amandus Johnson. Philadelphia: Swedish Colonial Society, 1925.

Logan, James, to Conrad Weiser, July 11, 1742. Peters Papers, 1697–1845, Historical Society of Pennsylvania, Philadelphia PA.

Logan, James, to William Penn, September 15, 1706. In *Correspondence between William Penn and James Logan*, edited by Edward Armstrong, 2:167–70. Philadelphia: Historical Society of Pennsylvania, 1872.

Marshall, Moses. "Examination of Indian Hannah alias Hannah Freeman," July 28, 1797. Chester County Historical Society, West Chester PA.

"Memorial to Humphry and Moses Marshall." Humphry and Moses Marshall Papers, William L. Clements Library, University of Michigan, Ann Arbor MI.

Minutes of the Board of Property, Oct 5, 1691. In *Pennsylvania Archives*, ser. 2, vol. 19, edited by William H. Egle, 72. Harrisburg: State Printer, 1890.

Minutes of the Directors of the Poor, 1800. Chester County Archives, West Chester PA.

Minutes of the Provincial Council of Pennsylvania. Vols. 5, 7. Philadelphia, 1851.

Miscellaneous Papers of the Pre-separation Meeting, Epistles, Records of the Philadelphia Yearly Meeting. Swarthmore College Library, Swarthmore, PA.

Mitchell, James T., and Henry Flanders. *The Statues at Large of Pennsylvania from 1682–1801*. Vol. 3. Harrisburg: State Printer, 1896–1915.

Moravian Indian Diaries, Philadelphia Barracks, 1764–1765. *Bethlehem Digital History Project*, 2011. http://bdhp.moravia.ed/community_records/christianindians/indiandiaryintro.html (accessed April 15, 2013).

Nelson, William, ed. *Documents relating to the Colonial History of the State of New Jersey*. 1st ser., vol. 20. Patterson: Call, 1880.

New Castle County, Del. Warrants and Surveys, 1679–1740. Historical Society of Pennsylvania, Philadelphia.

Papers of the Friendly Association for Regaining and Preserving Peace with the Indians by Pacific Measures. Vol. 1. Quaker Collection, Haverford College, Haverford PA.

Penn, William. "Additional Instructions to William Markham," 1681. In *William Penn and the Founding of America: A Documentary History*, edited by Jean Soderlund, 89. Philadelphia: University of Pennsylvania Press, 1983.

———. "Conditions or Concessions to the First Purchasers," July 11, 1681. In *William Penn and the Founding of America: A Documentary History*, edited by Jean Soderlund, 72–75. Philadelphia: University of Pennsylvania Press, 1983.

———. "A Further Account of the Province of Pennsylvania." In *Narratives of Early Pennsylvania, West New Jersey and Delaware, 1630–1707*, edited by Albert Cook Myers, 259–78. New York: Charles Scribner's Sons, 1912.

———. "Letter to the Free Society of Traders," August 16, 1683. In *William Penn and the Founding of America: A Documentary History*, edited by Jean Soderlund, 309–19. Philadelphia: University of Pennsylvania Press, 1983.

———. "Petition to Charles II," May 1680. In *William Penn and the Founding of America: A Documentary History*, edited by Jean Soderlund, 21–23. Philadelphia: University of Pennsylvania Press, 1983.

———. "Some Account of the Province of Pennsylvania." In *William Penn and the Founding of America: A Documentary History*, edited by Jean Soderlund, 58–65. Philadelphia: University of Pennsylvania Press, 1983.

———. "To the Inhabitants of Pennsylvania," April 8, 1681. In *William Penn and the Founding of America: A Documentary History*, edited by Jean Soderlund, 55. Philadelphia: University of Pennsylvania Press, 1983.

———. "To the Kings of the Indians." In *William Penn and the Founding of America: A Documentary History*, edited by Jean Soderlund, 86–88. Philadelphia: University of Pennsylvania Press, 1983.

Penn-Physick Papers, 1676–1804. Historical Society of Pennsylvania, Philadelphia.

Population Schedules of the First Census of the United States, 1790. Washington DC: U.S. Census Office, National Archives and Records Service, 1960.

Pratt, Richard H. *Proceedings of the National Conference of Charities and Correction at the Nineteenth Annual Session, Held in Denver, Colorado, June 23–29, 1892.* Edited by Isabel C. Barrows. Boston: George H. Ellis, 1892.

Prucha, Francis Paul, ed. *"William Penn" Essays and Other Writings.* Knoxville: University of Tennessee Press, 1981.

Quarter Sessions Indictments. Chester County Archives, West Chester PA.

"Records of the Kennett Monthly Meeting." Centre Preparative Meeting, Friends Historical Library, Swarthmore College, Swarthmore PA.

Ricord, Frederick W., ed. *Documents relating to the Colonial History of New Jersey.* Vol. 16. Trenton: John L. Murphy, 1891.

Saffron, Inga. "Wrecking Ball Threatens West Chester Boom." *Philadelphia Inquirer,* July 26, 2001.

Smith, John. "A Map of Virginia," 1612. In *The Complete Works of John Smith,* edited by Philip L. Barbour, 1:119. Chapel Hill: University of North Carolina Press, 1986.

Smith, Matthew, and James Gibson. "A Declaration and Remonstrance of the Distressed and Bleeding Frontier Inhabitants of the Province of Pennsylvania." In *The Paxton Papers,* edited by John R. Dunbar, 99–101. The Hague: Martinus Nijhoff, 1957.

Statements by Nathaniel Newlin and the Commissioner of Property on the Brandywine Indians' Complaint, 1726. Logan Family Papers, Indian Affairs, Historical Society of Pennsylvania, Philadelphia.

Sullivan, Thomas. "Before and After the Battle of Brandywine: Extracts from the Journal of Sergeant Thomas Sullivan." *Pennsylvania Magazine of History and Biography* 31, no. 4 (1907): 406–19.

Swann, Brian. *Coming to Light.* New York: Random House, 1994.

Taylor, Jacob, and Isaac Taylor. Papers, 1672–1775. Historical Society of Pennsylvania, Philadelphia.

Tetamie, Moses. "An Account of the Walking Purchase." Papers of the Friendly Association for Regaining and Preserving Peace with the Indians by Pacific Measures, vol. 1. Quaker Collections, Haverford College, Haverford PA.

Thomas, Gabriel. "An Historical and Geographical Account of Pensilvania and of West-New-Jersey," 1698. In *Narratives of Early Pennsylvania, West New Jersey and Delaware, 1630–1707,* edited by Albert Cook Myers. New York: Charles Scribner's Sons, 1912.

"Votes of the Assembly." In *Pennsylvania Archives,* ser. 8, vol. 2, edited by Gertrude MacKinney. Harrisburg, 1931–35.

"Votes of the Assembly." In *Pennsylvania Archives,* ser. 8, vol. 6, edited by Gertrude MacKinney. Harrisburg, 1931–35.

Wassenarer, Nicolaes van. "Historisch Verhael, 1624–1630." In *Narratives of New Netherland, 1609–1664,* edited by J. Franklin Jameson. New York: Charles Scribner's Sons, 1909.

"West Chester." *Commercial Herald,* June 28, 1834, 13, 26.

Williams, Roger. *A Key into the Language of North America.* London: Gregory Dexter, 1643.

Winter, J. L. Newspaper clipping, March 21, 1909. Indian File, Chester County Historical Society, West Chester PA.

Secondary Sources

Becker, Marshall J. "Hannah Freeman: An Eighteenth-Century Lenape Living among Colonial Farmers." *Pennsylvania Magazine of History and Biography* 114, no. 2 (1990): 249–69.